SPIRITUAL JAVA

BOOKS BY BILL JOHNSON

A Life of Miracles

Dreaming With God

Face to Face

Here Comes Heaven

Release the Power of Jesus

Strengthen Yourself in the Lord

The Supernatural Power of a Transformed Mind

The Supernatural Power of a Transformed Mind 40 Day Devotional

When Heaven Invades Earth

When Heaven Invades Earth 40 Day Devotional

AVAILABLE FROM DESTINY IMAGE PUBLISHERS

BILL JOHNSON•BENI JOHNSON
KRIS VALLOTTON•KEVIN DEDMON
DANNY SILK•BANNING LIEBSCHER

SPIRITUAL JAVA

DESTINY IMAGE® PUBLISHERS, INC.

P.O. Box 310, Shippensburg, PA 17257-0310

"Speaking to the Purposes of God for This Generation and for the Generations to Come."

This book and all other Destiny Image, Revival Press, MercyPlace, Fresh Bread, Destiny Image Fiction, and Treasure House books are available at Christian bookstores and distributors worldwide.

For a U.S. bookstore nearest you, call 1-800-722-6774.
For more information on foreign distributors, call 717-532-3040.
Reach us on the Internet: www.destinyimage.com.

Trade Paper ISBN 13: 978-0-7684-3285-5
Hardcover ISBN 13: 978-0-7684-3487-3
Large Print ISBN 13: 978-0-7684-3488-0
Ebook ISBN 13: 978-0-7684-9085-5

For Worldwide Distribution, Printed in the U.S.A.
3 4 5 6 7 8 9 10 11 / 13 12 11

Contents

Introduction 9

Chapter 1: *Aggressive Faith* (Bill Johnson) 11

Chapter 2: *Getting Into the Flow of Grace* (Banning Liebscher) 17

Chapter 3: *Creating a Safe Place* (Danny Silk) 23

Chapter 4: *Where Did Your Storm Come From?* (Bill Johnson) 29

Chapter 5: *Increasing in Favor* (Bill Johnson) 35

Chapter 6: *Forget, but Don't Forget* (Kris Vallotton) 41

Chapter 7: *Joy* (Beni Johnson) 47

Chapter 8: *Transformed by Promotion* (Bill Johnson) 53

Chapter 9: *Friends and Co-Laborers* (Bill Johnson) 59

Chapter 10: *Just Do It!* (Kevin Dedmon) 65

Chapter 11: *Light Therapy* (Kevin Dedmon) 71

Chapter 12: *Living Under the Influence* (Bill Johnson) 77

Chapter 13: *Calling Forth His Desires* (Beni Johnson) 83

Chapter 14: *God Is Always Speaking* (Kris Vallotton) 89

Chapter 15:   *Character—With Power* (Bill Johnson)............................. 95

Chapter 16:   *Kingdom Increase* (Banning Liebscher)............................ 101

Chapter 17:   *Praying in the Spirit* (Bill Johnson) 107

Chapter 18:   *Becoming Children of Light* (Danny Silk) 113

Chapter 19:   *Pursuing Your Destiny* (Kris Vallotton) 119

Chapter 20:   *When God Colors Outside the Lines* (Bill Johnson).............. 125

Chapter 21:   *One Hundred Percent Success* (Kevin Dedmon) 131

Chapter 22:   *Divine Encounters* (Bill Johnson) 137

Chapter 23:   *Connection With God* (Beni Johnson) 143

Chapter 24:   *Light in Unlikely Places* (Banning Liebscher)...................... 149

Chapter 25:   *Like Father, Like Son and Daughter* (Bill Johnson) 155

Chapter 26:   *Thanksgiving—Agreeing With Heaven* (Bill Johnson).......... 161

Chapter 27:   *Combat Darkness with Joyful Worship* (Beni Johnson)......... 167

Chapter 28:   *Drawing on the Grace of God* (Danny Silk) 173

Chapter 29:   *Smeared With God* (Bill Johnson)..................................... 179

Chapter 30:   *Practicing the Gifts of the Spirit* (Kris Vallotton) 185

Chapter 31:   *Green Light District* (Bill Johnson)..................................... 191

Chapter 32:   *True Humility* (Kris Vallotton) 197

Chapter 33:   *It's Easy to Hear From God* (Kevin Dedmon)..................... 203

Chapter 34: *God Hides Things for You, Not From You* (Bill Johnson) 209

Chapter 35: *If It Matters to You, It Matters to Him* (Bill Johnson).......... 215

Chapter 36: *The Name of Jesus* (Kevin Dedmon) 221

Chapter 37: *Bringing Signs and Wonders to the Streets* (Bill Johnson)...... 227

Chapter 38: *Strength From Covenant People* (Bill Johnson) 233

Chapter 39: *First Love* (Banning Liebscher) 239

Chapter 40: *Welcoming His Visitation* (Bill Johnson) 245

Introduction

BILL JOHNSON

I was standing in the airport in chilly Vancouver, Canada, with Mike, an associate from Bethel Church in Redding, California. We were waiting in line at Starbucks (one of my favorite places). As I stood there in anticipation of a hot cup of coffee, enjoying the familiar aromas, sights, and sounds of the coffee shop, I noticed that Mike was taking a long time with the cashier. It didn't occur to me that anything important was happening. I was simply there getting coffee as we waited for our next flight.

Then I saw him take the cashier's hand, and they closed their eyes and bowed their heads in prayer. When they had finished, Mike joined me and explained what had just happened. As he was ordering, he had seen a spirit of suicide on the cashier, so he began to minister to her to break that power. She told him, "God sent you in here today."

I was caught off guard. All I had been thinking about was coffee! I had momentarily forgotten the more important things in life. It's easy to do that. Our minds stray into natural thinking only, our faith erodes so subtly that we don't notice it happening, and little by little we can begin to think "practically," leaning on natural wisdom instead of Kingdom reality.

Habakkuk 2:2 says, *"Write the vision and make it plain on tablets, that he may run who reads it."* People need motivation to run. That's the main reason I travel and speak and write as much as I can. I want to give other people the fuel they need to get up and go. I want them to have whatever revelation I have, just as I feed on the revelation given to me by others. To participate in the active, awesome work of the Kingdom, we can't casually row, row, row our boat gently down the stream. We've got to run!

I do as Habakkuk advised. I write down God's ideas about my life whenever they are revealed to me. I mark up and underline my Bible every which way. I write down prophecies I've received on note cards and in my computer, and I carry those with me wherever I go. I put Post-It notes on the dashboard of my car. I post them all over the church sometimes so that when I walk around and pray I see notes everywhere, reminding me of what God is saying. I keep a journal for my children and my grandchildren that they might see what God did in my lifetime. We even have a staff member at our church whose entire job description is to record the miracles that happen in and through our church and with our ministry teams. I want people to know the great and mighty works of the Lord long after we're gone, so they can run with the vision even further.

Of course, a written record is only useful when you review it. *Re* means "to go back," and *view* means "to see." *Go back* over God's promises until you can *see*! This is not simply positive thinking or using your imagination to trick yourself into believing some alternate reality. It's meditating on what God has said until you can see it and run with it. It's telling each other the true God-stories that tend to fade if we don't review them. The testimony of what the Lord has done helps us to remember who God is, what His covenant is like, and who He intends to be in our lives. Every testimony of His work in someone's life is a prophecy for those with ears to hear.

Several of my associates at Bethel Church and I have compiled this book because we wanted to distill for you the spiritual wealth we have shared over the past years in many settings. It is as if we have brewed a pot of rich coffee for you. Each time you enjoy a few more sips, you will be warmed and energized to step out into your world with renewed spiritual effectiveness. As you read and consider each of these short chapters, may every one of them be like spiritual java for your soul.

Chapter 1

Aggressive Faith
Bill Johnson

THE HOLY SPIRIT LIVES in my spirit and in yours. That is our place of communion with God. As we learn to receive from our spirits, we learn how to be Spirit-led. As we open ourselves up to the Holy Spirit within us, we learn how to operate by faith. *"By faith, we understand"* (Heb. 11:3).

"Faith comes by hearing" (Rom. 10:17), not from having heard. It is the listening heart, in the present tense, that is ready for Heaven's deposit of faith. The whole nature of faith implies a relationship with God that is current. The emphasis is on hearing—in the now!

I'm sure that you have had the experience of reading the Bible, and a verse jumps out at you. It gives life and encouragement to you, yet earlier you couldn't teach about or explain that verse at all. What happened is this: Your spirit received the life-giving power of the Word from the Holy Spirit (see 2 Cor. 3:6).

As you learn to receive from your spirit, your mind becomes the student and is therefore subject to the Holy Spirit. Through the process of revelation and the exercise of faith, your mind eventually obtains understanding. Faith reflects the realities of God's world into ours. Faith is the substance of the unseen realm (see Heb. 11:1).

If I go into the local pizza parlor and order a pizza, I get a receipt and a number that I am to display in a conspicuous place on my table. A stranger may come to my table and announce that nobody's going to give me any pizza. But I can just point to the number and tell him, "When pizza number 52 is done, it is mine!" That number is the *substance* of the pizza hoped for. If that guy tells me that my number isn't any good, I can just point to my receipt. It verifies the value of the number. When my pizza is done, the waiter will look around for my number and he'll bring it to me.

How does the product of Heaven know where to land? He looks for the substance—the number. Faith is the currency of Heaven. My reward has been paid for. My receipt (contained in the Bible) verifies my right to both the number and the reward.

That kind of faith is aggressive by nature. It has focus and purpose. It grabs hold of the reality of the Kingdom and forcefully, even violently, brings it into a collision with this natural, inferior, earthly kingdom, which cannot stand against it. *"The kingdom of heaven suffers violence, and the violent take it by force"* (Matt. 11:12).

That does not mean that our faith needs to be loud. Devils know the difference between people who are bold and aggressive because of their faith and those who are simply covering their fears with aggressive behavior. Christians often try to cover their immaturity and fear when casting out devils—yelling threats, calling on angels for help, waving their hands, and more.

But our authority comes from real faith, which is found in rest. Peaceful rest is the climate that faith grows in. (See Hebrews 3:11-4:11.) It is the Prince of Peace who will soon crush satan underneath our feet! (See Romans 16:20.) Hearts (spirits) that find rest in Him can prevail over whatever does not originate with the Prince of Peace.

Two blind men who sat by the road called out to Jesus. People told them to be quiet. That only hardened their desperate determination; they cried out all the louder. He called them forth and healed them, and He attributed their miracle to their faith. (See Matthew 9:27.)

A woman who had hemorrhaged for 12 years pressed through a crowd. When she was able finally to touch the garment of Jesus, she was healed. He attributed her healing to her faith. (See Matthew 9:20-22.)

The stories of this kind are many, all with similar endings—people are healed or delivered because of their persistent faith. Whether faith cries out very loudly or it quietly strengthens people to press forward, faith-actions always seem violent in the spirit world. Faith grabs hold of an invisible, superior reality—and it won't let go.

Our faith has its anchor in the unseen realm. It lives from the invisible toward the visible. Our faith actualizes what it realizes. Our faith provides eyes for our hearts and minds.

We need to understand that Jesus expects people to see from their hearts. He once called a group of religious leaders hypocrites because they could discern the weather but could not discern the times (see Matt. 16:2-4). They claimed to be spiritual leaders, and yet they could not discern spiritual matters with their hearts. They had become blind to His dominion because of their own corrupted hearts. Jesus judged their faith to be hypocritical.

A heart that does not see is a hard heart (see Mark 8:17-18). Our born-again experience enables us to see from the heart (see John 3:3), and thereby to apply what we see with confident faith. Our faith was never intended only to get us into the family of God. Rather, it is the *nature* of life in this family. Faith sees. It brings His Kingdom into focus. All of the Father's resources, all of His benefits, are accessible through faith.

To encourage us in our capacity to see, Jesus gave specific instructions: *"Seek first the kingdom of God"* (Matt. 6:33). He told His followers that He did only what He saw His Father do (see John 5:19). Paul taught us, *"Set your mind on things above, not on things on the earth"* (Col. 3:2). He also stated, *"For the things which are seen are temporary, but the things which are not seen are eternal"* (2 Cor. 4:18). These words instruct us to turn our attention toward the invisible.

Such insights are vital for those who want more.

Points to Ponder

1. What does it look like when you exercise aggressive faith? What hinders your living by faith? What helps you live by faith?

....

....

....

2. Jesus expects people to see from their hearts, and He says that a heart that does not see is a hard heart. In His words:

   Is your heart still hardened? Having eyes, do you not see? And having ears, do you not hear? And do you not remember? (Mark 8:17b-18)

....

....

....

3. How does your own heart most often become hardened? How does that make your faith lapse into passivity? How do you tend to miss His voice? What can you do about it?

....

....

....

....

Meditation

Rest. Rest awhile in the presence of the Life-giving One who is the Lord of your spirit, soul, and body. Regardless of how much your current circumstances may have distracted you from God, you *can* stop thinking your own thoughts and start living by faith. His Spirit will help you.

He will *"keep him in perfect peace, whose mind is stayed on"* Him (Isa. 26:3). Listen to His voice, not to your worries. Trust in Him, not in your fears. Allow the continual influence of His transforming Kingdom to flow through your spirit.

Chapter 2

Getting Into the Flow of Grace
Banning Liebscher

I HAVE HEARD IT said that grace is "God's empowerment to do what we are called to do." What a great description. When grace is in your life, there's a power to do what's on your heart. Whether it's writing books, preaching, running a business, or living a life of holiness, it's grace that makes it possible. When I am properly aligned under the leaders God has placed in my life, grace flows freely. This principle is pictured in Psalm 133:1-2:

> *Behold, how good and how pleasant it is for brethren to dwell together in unity! It is like the precious oil upon the head, running down on the beard, the beard of Aaron, running down on the edge of his garments.*

Unity speaks of proper alignment, and oil speaks of the anointing of the Holy Spirit—of grace. When I align myself under spiritual authority, a level of grace begins to flow in my life, because the oil that is flowing from the head starts to run all over me. I feel a wind pushing me forward. Let me remind you of First Peter 5:5: *"Likewise you younger people, submit yourselves to your elders. Yes, all of you be submissive to one another, and be clothed with humility, for 'God resists the proud, but gives **grace*** *to the humble*'" (emphasis added). There is a grace that comes from being under covering.

As a kid, I used to love Slip 'N Slides. Recently, we bought our kids their first Slip 'N Slide. What a blast! But this one was way cooler than any I had played on as a kid. It had two slides side-by-side for two children to race each other. A perfect arch of water squirted out from the middle to cover the ride, which ended in a small pool of water backed by an inflatable cushion. This Slip 'N Slide was high tech! My wife and I just laughed and laughed as we delighted in our three kids scooting down in glee— over and over. It looked like so much fun that the two of us were wondering if people in their thirties could still negotiate the Slip 'N Slide.

Slip 'N Slides are a blast, that is, when they have water on them. Without H_2O, they are a completely different experience—not fun. Imagine running at full speed, launching forward into a perfect horizontal position in the air, and landing on a Slip 'N Slide with no water. Ouch! Living life without grace is like diving onto a Slip 'N Slide with no water. I see many people who, because they aren't under covering, are trying to live life without grace. They always feel as if there is a wind resisting them as they attempt to move forward. They feel as if they were meant to fly but can never get off the ground.

There are people who sit in my office and tell me that the devil is resisting them and they can't figure out why. But sometimes it's not the devil hindering them; it's God resisting them. They have refused to submit their lives to covering, so God is resisting the pride in them. It is not a good idea to have God hinder you. Yet I have seen firsthand that when someone harnesses the revelation of covering and submits to spiritual authority, the wind shifts in that person's life. Instead of resistance, he feels the wind accelerating him toward his destiny.

When you get into the flow of grace, you will see definite benefits in your life. One is courage. God is calling us to do the impossible, to be world-changers, and we will never be able to follow His lead without the courage He supplies. Queen Esther needed courage to do what she was called to do in her day. It was because of the input of her cousin Mordecai, who had become like a father to her when her parents died, that she received the courage necessary to fulfill every part of her destiny. As a result, a nation was saved from death.

Another benefit of grace is wisdom. The Book of Proverbs is filled with encouragement to pursue and value wisdom, and a significant number of these exhortations were given to a son by his father. One of the main ways this inheritance of wisdom shows up is in the ability to learn from the mistakes and successes of our fathers and mothers in the faith. I want to learn from those who are older and wiser than I am. Some things I will have to ascertain on my own, but I want to soak in as much wisdom as I can from the older generation.

Protection is another clear benefit of walking humbly under the covering of your elders. The spirit of independence has separated too many people from community, and the enemy's darts are raining down on them. It's not really that complicated. If it's raining and you don't want to get wet, then jump under an umbrella.

Another benefit of getting under the right kind of "rain," the reign of grace, is that doing so provides you with a strong identity. Knowing who you are in God produces security, and that security produces confidence. Most of my ministry over the years has been targeted toward youth and young adults. Because of that, most of my teaching about grace and covering has emphasized the importance of the younger generation honoring the older. But Malachi mentions the hearts of the fathers turning to their children—and the hearts of the children turning to the fathers (see Mal. 4:6). Honor must flow in both directions. Both generations need each other. Like a team competing to win a relay race, we must understand how to hand off the baton. We don't want to experience a great outpouring of the Holy Spirit but not know how to pass on the baton successfully.

Grace is flowing down. Are you under the flow?

Points to Ponder

1. Have you ever thought before about how the flow of grace works? Did you realize that so much of God's grace must flow through the people He has placed over us? Whom has He placed over you to help supply you with courage, wisdom, protection, and identity?

    ....

    ....

    ....

2. Have you had the experience of meeting God's resistance instead of receiving His grace? What was it like? What did you do about it?

    ....

    ....

    ....

3. Can you identify in your own experience a time when you chose to "get under the umbrella"? What was it like? Do you think that you are still covered by an umbrella of grace today?

    ....

    ....

    ....

Meditation

Using the eyes of your heart, look around you. Paul prayed that *"the eyes of your understanding"* would be *"enlightened; that you may know what is the hope of His calling, what are the riches of the glory of His inheritance in the saints"* (Eph. 1:18).

Meditate on the relationships in your life and what your "inheritance in the saints" consists of. With the help of the Holy Spirit, see if you can discern His grace in your life in the form of courage, wisdom, protection, and identity. Ask God to help you situate yourself more fully in the flow of His grace.

Chapter 3

CREATING A SAFE PLACE
Danny Silk

GOD, THE CREATOR OF the whole universe, created people to be free. In fact, He specifically *trusted* His people with freedom. C.S. Lewis presented a concise account of the situation in *Mere Christianity*:

> God created things which had free will. That means creatures which can go either wrong or right. Some people think they can imagine a creature which was free but had no possibility of going wrong; I cannot. If a thing is free to be good it is also free to be bad. And free will is what has made evil possible. Why, then, did God give them free will? Because free will, though it makes evil possible, is also the only thing that makes possible any love or goodness or joy worth having a world of automata—of creatures that worked like machines—would hardly be worth creating. The happiness which God designs for His higher creatures is the happiness of being freely, voluntarily united to Him and to each other in an ecstasy of love and delight compared with which the most rapturous love between a man and a woman on this earth is mere milk and water. And for that they must be free.

Of course God knew what would happen if they used their freedom the wrong way: apparently He thought it worth the risk.[1]

The difficulty in leading free people is *risk*—the risk that they could use their freedom the wrong way. Unlike God, too many of us in the Church do not understand why the risk is worth it. The threat of misused freedom looms larger than the prize of true freedom. And because of that, we get scared. This fear can become endemic in supposedly free societies. In the United States, which is the supposed leader of the so-called "free world," fear is rampant. We as believers need to tap into some pretty powerful stuff if we are going to resist the fear in our culture and supersede it, extending trust to God and to people. We certainly need to pound Heaven's value for freedom into our own belief systems.

When we use our freedom to love as intended, as Lewis pointed out, our own freedom and joy and that of the people around us will be protected and cultivated. Leaders need to accomplish many things, from defining reality to reaching productive goals. But the priority of Heaven is crystal clear, *"If you have not love…you're just noisy"* (see 1 Cor. 13:1). Leaders who extinguish love in the process of reaching goals have achieved earth's priorities, maybe. But the higher goals of Heaven require us to cultivate and preserve love, and thus to cultivate and preserve freedom, for you cannot have love without freedom. God is love, and His Kingdom is a Kingdom of freedom.

When God shows up, people feel free. If that is not happening, we should wonder why. Why is freedom not breaking out in more places? Could it be because a lot of people, including leaders, misunderstand the goal of God's leadership in our lives?

I propose that the goal of God's leadership in our lives is to create a *safe place* for us to discover who we are and why we are here. A safe place is a place where the fear of misused freedom does not get to rise up and intimidate us out of risking trust and love in our relationships with one another. A safe place is what gets cultivated when freedom is expressed through love, because the essence of love is *safety* and *connection*.

Now most people think God wants us to line up, stay in line, and be good. We have embraced the idea that He is patient, but still on the verge of anger. But consider what God said through the prophet Isaiah: *"The mountains and hills will be removed, but My kindness shall never leave you, nor shall My covenant of peace with you ever be removed"* (see Isa. 54:10). God is underlining the fact that He is *not* unpredictable. He is saying, in essence, that He is in a perpetual good mood. He wants us to have a blessed assurance. He wants us to know that, with Him in charge, the place is safe, and we can relax into the freedom that comes to us when Jesus shows up. This truth would seem to be a no-brainer, especially since Jesus came and introduced the New Covenant a couple thousand years ago. We should be getting this by now.

Our covenant with God puts us in a safe place. We human beings blossom in a safe place. The nourishing effects of His presence bring us into completeness.

God has put this little gland inside our brains called the *amygdala*. It is an almond-shaped mass of nuclei located deep within our temporal lobes. This gland is important for determining our emotional responses, especially those associated with fear. As soon as something threatening happens, your amygdala kicks on and begins to flood your body with messages such as: *React! Defend! Flee! Fight!*

It does not take a rocket scientist to discover that people who are scared out of their wits are not at their creative best. Just see what happens if you try to rescue a drowning person who is thrashing around in a panic; be careful, or you may be in danger yourself.

But when people are in a safe place where other people carry the *shalom* of Heaven, grace and peace and trust and mutual love will flourish. The leadership structure sustains the flow of heavenly reality. Confidence and acceptance are communicated. Before long, the potential anointings and creativity of the people start to rise to the surface, and people will find room to manifest their gifts in the life of the church. Miracles, signs, and wonders will occur in a sustained way. Spiritual shackles will fall off. Then people will start to change the world with the Kingdom of Heaven that they carry.

Endnote

1. C.S. Leswis, *Mere Christianity* (New York: Harper Collins, 2001), 47-48.

Points to Ponder

1. As you look back over your life, what "unsafe" times can you identify? What about times that were safe? Correlate your sense of well-being with the sense of safety that you felt.

    ....

    ....

    ....

2. "Connect the dots" in your experiences. How has safety enhanced emotions and motivations such as joy, peace, and creativity? How has *un*safety caused you to withdraw into yourself? (For example, consider the last time you were sick or injured and ask yourself how capable you felt to reach out lovingly to others.)

    ....

    ....

    ....

3. Is your church a safe place? Your workplace? Your family home? How are you in a position to improve the level of safety in any of those places?

    ....

    ....

    ....

Meditation

Where are you right now? Are you in a safe place? Can you identify your dominant emotions and thought patterns well enough to bring them to your Father in the simple trust that He is *for* you?

Ask Him to calm your soul and spirit. Once you are more peaceful inside (and maybe you were already peaceful inside), ask Him what He has in mind for you right now. "Receiving mode or giving mode, Lord?"

Ask Him to lead you *"by still waters"* (see Ps. 23), and to sustain you in safe places, so that you will have the inner resources you need when you are in scary situations.

Chapter 4

Where Did Your Storm Come From?
BILL JOHNSON

THE STORMS OF LIFE can present terrific challenges and opportunities for us to grow. But it makes a great deal of difference which kind of storm you're in. Some storms, though sent by the devil, can provoke us and invite us to use the revelation we already have. They are miracles waiting to happen, as in this passage from Mark 4:35-41:

On the same day, when evening had come, He said to them, "Let us cross over to the other side." Now when they had left the multitude, they took Him along in the boat as He was. And other little boats were also with Him. And a great windstorm arose, and the waves beat into the boat, so that it was already filling. But He was in the stern, asleep on a pillow. And they awoke Him and said to Him, "Teacher, do You not care that we are perishing?" Then He arose and rebuked the wind, and said to the sea, "Peace, be still!" And the wind ceased and there was a great calm. But He said to them, "Why are you so fearful? How is it that you have no faith?" And they feared exceedingly, and said to one another, "Who can this be, that even the wind and the sea obey Him!"

But there are other kinds of storms God sends to show us we're going in the wrong direction, like this familiar one:

> *But the Lord sent out a great wind on the sea, and there was a mighty tempest on the sea, so that the ship was about to be broken up. Then the mariners were afraid; and every man cried out to his god, and threw the cargo that was in the ship into the sea, to lighten the load. But Jonah had gone down into the lowest parts of the ship, had lain down, and was fast asleep. So the captain came to him, and said to him, "What do you mean, sleeper? Arise, call on your God; perhaps your God will consider us, so that we may not perish"* (Jonah 1:4-6).

We see in these passages two storms, and two different purposes for each storm. One was sent by God, the other by the devil. Each situation involved a man sleeping in the boat, one because of depression and a way of escaping his unpleasant reality, the other because He was living from the Kingdom toward earth, and in the Kingdom there was no storm.

The question is, which storm are you in? And are you dealing with it the way God wants you to deal with it? Have you let past miracles "tutor" you to a place of faith adequate for your current challenges?

The disciples' storm was sent by the devil to keep them from the will of God. Jonah's storm was sent by God to turn him back to the will of God. Some people face storms because they took a left when God took a right. God brings a storm in His mercy to drive them back. Others face storms *because they are in the middle of God's will*. He doesn't like the storm, but He wants to train you to use tools He's given you to calm it.

Most of us find ourselves in a storm and instantly conclude our job is to cry out to God to intervene. But the purpose of the storm is not to make us cry out like that. God never allows a storm without first providing the tools to calm the storm. He wants us to use those tools to bring about a miraculous result. He rebuked His disciples for lacking faith.

"Wait a minute!" they might have thought, "We just had enough faith to come and wake you up. And You did what we asked. Isn't that how it's supposed to work?" Apparently not. Jesus implied that it was their responsibility to command the storm to cease.

We are no different. Our prayers involve trying to get God to fix problems on earth. Maybe we should be commanding the storms to be calm. Maybe we should be seeing situations from Heaven's perspective and declaring the word of the Lord so that we can watch Heaven invade earth.

I have tremendous love and respect for the ministry of intercession, as I am married to a great intercessor. But many intercessors moan and groan and weep and are depressed all the time and call that "intercession." They never come into a place of faith when they pray.

I know what that is like. There have been seasons in my life when I prayed great lengths of time, very diligently, very disciplined, very impressive if I had counted the hours. God never penalized me for it because He knew the sincerity of my heart. But in reality, of the time I spent praying, very little of it was in faith. Most of it was in depression, discouragement, or "burden."

The tragedy is that many believers can't yet distinguish the difference between the burden of the Lord and the weight of their own unbelief.

The worse some people feel when they're through praying, the more they feel gratified to be an anointed intercessor. It's OK to start there, but do whatever is necessary to arrive at a place of faith. Then you will be able to see situations from the perspective of Heaven—and you will be able to bring Heaven to earth with a simple word or two.

You shouldn't have to seek God in hours of discouraged prayer. The time to pray is beforehand, as Jesus did, crying out to God in private times when nothing is going wrong. That's how to store up power and create an inner atmosphere of peace and faith that you take with you into the troubling situation.

Let's not waste our miracles, either. Let's not watch God do something awesome, then give a little golf clap, a little "amen," and walk away unchanged.

Points to Ponder

1. Think of the greatest conflict or crisis in your life in the past year. See if you can identify the tools that God put into your life to help you take care of that problem. In what ways might He have been using the circumstance to equip you for the future?

....

....

....

2. Some teachers say that God likes to wait until the last minute to intervene and show His sovereignty. They think that's His cute and clever way of showing He was in control the whole time. You hear people say, "God's never early or late, but He's always right on time." If He always intervenes at the last minute, it's often because we aren't using the tools we've been given in the first place. Think about that one!

....

....

....

Meditation

God allows problems into your life so you can defeat them—not only so that you can cry out to Him for deliverance every time. The tools will be in the boat with you, although the enemy will fan the winds of fear to get you to forget where the tools are.

Most of us can identify with the disciples on the stormy sea. We might even applaud them for doing the right thing when they cried out, "Save us! Don't you know we are perishing?" But Jesus turned to them and asked them why they did not have any faith.

In the midst of your storm, stir up your faith in the One who will show you where you put your tools. Regardless of where your storm came from, you have been trained for this moment. You *do* know what to do.

Chapter 5

Increasing in Favor
Bill Johnson

SOME OF US WHO have been raised in a democratic society may struggle with the idea that God gives more favor to some people than others.

God's favor is not the same as His love. You cannot do anything to change the vastness of God's love for you. But even Jesus Himself had to grow *"in favor with God and man"* (Luke 2:52). This verse amazes me. I can understand that fact that He needed to grow in favor with man, but why did He have to grow in favor with His Father God? He was perfect in every way.

The answer lies in the fact that Jesus did everything He did *as a man*, laying His divinity aside, in order to be a model for us. Therefore He, like any of us, had to be tested. At baptism, He received His anointing from the Spirit. But instead of launching right into His ministry, He was led by the Spirit into the wilderness. There He was tested by the enemy, specifically in the area of the word that had just been spoken over Him. If you look at the account of Jesus' temptation in Luke, you'll notice that He went into the wilderness *"filled with the Holy Spirit"* and He returned *"in the power of the Spirit"* (Luke 4:1,14). Because He passed the test, the favor to walk in His potential was released in a greater measure.

As Jesus modeled, each of us must grow in favor if we are going to fulfill our destiny in God. But favor, because it is so glorious and powerful, is weighty. Thus God, in His mercy, gives us His favor in the measure our character can handle, taking us from glory to glory, faith to faith, and strength to strength.

If we are going to develop the character to fulfill our potential as kings and priests in the Kingdom, we must grow in our ability to strengthen ourselves in the Lord. When the Amalekites attacked the city of Ziklag, David and his men were away. They returned to discover only the smoking ashes of the city—their unprotected wives and children and goods had been captured. Insane with grief and fury, they threatened to stone David to death.

But David regained their favor and went on to lead them in victory.

Now David was greatly distressed, for the people spoke of stoning him, because the soul of all the people was grieved, every man for his sons and his daughters. But David strengthened himself in the Lord his God (1 Samuel 30:6).

It worked. His men rallied under him, and together they tracked down the Amalekites and retrieved what was theirs.

How can we learn this vital ability to strengthen and minister to ourselves? We need to recognize that when David sought the Lord and strengthened himself at Ziklag, that was not the first time He had done so. He possessed the initiative to succeed in the midst of a desperate situation at Ziklag because he had been seeking the Lord for years. He had sought God in the secret place, when nobody was watching. He had rallied himself time and time again when humanly speaking the situation was grim.

We may be able to experience God's strength through positive peer pressure and the momentum of a corporate move of God's glory, but what will happen to us when we have nothing to rely on? God knew David would succeed as a leader because he exhibited the same quality of maturity that God is looking for in us. People who can "land on their feet" when everything turns upside down have developed spiritual longevity. They have not been taken out by burnout or moral failure. They have adhered firmly to their God through thick and thin.

Now let me be clear that learning to strengthen ourselves does not mean that we develop an independent lifestyle. Our lifestyle as believers must remain focused on serving, loving, and leaning on each other in the Body of Christ. But for the sake of becoming mature and growing in favor so that we can bless those around us, God brings moments into our lives when we have to stand alone in difficulty and testing. God will even blind the eyes and deafen the ears of our closest friends in those moments—so we can learn to minister to ourselves.

Don't blame your friends for failing you in a hard time. Understand God's priorities and be a "quick learner." God wants to put new tools into your hands (at least they will be new to you). He wants you to become a mature believer who thinks and acts like Him out of your own free will. Mature believers are those He can trust with the secrets of His heart because they will not use the favor He gives for their own purposes, but rather for His.

David's life was not set down in Scripture merely to inspire us. We only need to read the accounts of his sins to know that he was not some kind of superhero. His life is really a call to every believer. If one man who was a sinner, who lived hundreds of years before the blood of Jesus was shed, could come into that place of favor with God, then how much more should those who are covered by that blood be able to come into an even greater destiny—to be like Christ and to finish His work on the planet?

You and I are seated in Christ in heavenly places (see Eph. 2:6). If Jesus is currently seated on the throne of David, then so are we! We have delegated authority to establish His Kingdom wherever the sole of our foot treads. But while God calls us "kings," the degree to which we walk in that position is still a matter of potential. And God is not responsible for making us reach our potential. It requires our participation.

Points to Ponder

1. Explain in your own words the statement: "God's favor is not the same as His love." Why did Jesus Himself have to grow *"in favor with God and man"* (Luke 2:52), just as we do?

    ....

    ....

    ....

2. Why do you have to be tested?

    ....

    ....

    ....

3. Can you remember a time when you did what David did—you strengthened yourself in the Lord? Was it recent or a long time ago? What have you done in between crises to ensure that you will be able to strengthen yourself in the Lord next time you are hit with adversity?

    ....

    ....

    ....

Meditation

Make it your intention to go to a "secret place" sometime today, and to acknowledge who God is. Exalt Him, and find some Scripture that strengthens your personal identity as His son or daughter. You could start with this one, the song sung in Heaven:

*You were slain, and have redeemed us to God by Your blood out of every tribe and tongue and people and nation, and have made us **kings and priests** to our God; and we shall reign on the earth* (Revelation 5:9-10, emphasis added).

Keep it up as often as you can, so that when your times of testing come, you will be ready.

Chapter 6

FORGET, BUT DON'T FORGET
KRIS VALLOTTON

AMPUTEES COMMONLY EXPERIENCE SOMETHING called "phantom" pain or sensation, when their nervous system and brain mistakenly interpret that certain physical signals are being sent by a limb that is no longer attached to their body. Sometimes they feel that their amputated arm or leg is still there. They feel everything from dull aches to sharp, shooting pains, as well as the sensation of throbbing or burning. It is no fun; it seems so real. Amputees have to remind themselves that the pain is imaginary.

The memories of your sinful past can be like those phantom pains, only it can be a little trickier because at your conversion you did not lose only a part of yourself; you literally died and were raised from the dead:

> *Therefore we were buried with Him through baptism into death, that just as Christ was raised from the dead by the glory of the Father, even so we also should walk in newness of life. For if we have been united together in the likeness of His death, certainly we also shall be in the likeness of His resurrection, knowing this, that our old man was*

crucified with Him, that the body of sin might be done away with, that we should no longer be slaves of sin. For he who has died has been freed from sin (Romans 6:4-7).

How can you retrain your brain to think and remember in accordance with that new reality? There are a number of truths that we all need to interact with regularly so that the reality of our conversion becomes established in our thinking and manifests fully in our behavior. Invite the Holy Spirit to make these familiar ideas fresh, revealing new layers of this great, mysterious salvation that we have received, and to take that revelation beyond mere head knowledge into a deeper level of freedom and power.

First, consider what Peter declared to the people after the healing of the lame man at the Beautiful Gate: *"Repent therefore and be converted, that your sins may be blotted out"* (Acts 3:19). The record of your sinful past is blotted out—completely erased—when you repented and were converted.

Scripture also puts it another way, telling us that at your conversion you entered into a covenant with God through the blood of Jesus, and that one of the foundational realities of this covenant, prophesied by Jeremiah, was: *"Their sins and their lawless deeds **I will remember no more"*** (Heb. 10:17, emphasis added).

If your sin has been blotted out and forgotten by God, then what are you to do with your memories? How can you review your past through the blood of Jesus and not apart from it? It comes down to a choice of whose voice to listen to.

The devil, on the one hand, has kept meticulous records of your past. Yet those reminders are powerless without your agreement. The devil is the "accuser of the brethren," whereas Jesus is your defender. Whenever you look at your past apart from the blood of Jesus, you end up agreeing with the devil. Your agreement emboldens and empowers him, and he sets upon you to devour you. On the other hand, whenever you agree with God, you shake free from the power of the lie. When you agree with God, you step into the power of truth.

The devil remembers your sin. God has forgotten it. Which spiritual reality—one heavenly, one hellish—are you going to agree with? The results of your choice will manifest themselves in your life.

According to Paul, you must *"reckon [yourself] to be dead to sin but alive to God in Jesus Christ our Lord"* (Rom. 6:11). The evidence of this new reality must not be assessed from your individual behavior, but rather from what Jesus did for you on the cross.

Being told to think of yourself as dead to sin is more than a suggestion to think positively about your conversion. It is an invitation to step into the reality of true freedom. Forgiveness, in effect, changes the past. The blood of Jesus actually changes your history into His story. Such is the love of God; what was once despised becomes a testimony of God's grace and a thing of beauty.

Does forgetting your sin sound like an impossible assignment? It is, without the empowerment of God. But when you decide to agree with God's perspective on your sin, He gives you the grace to forget those things that seem so bad and unforgettable. He also gives you grace to remember what is true about you, now that you are His. Here are a couple of Scriptures about it (I have added the emphasis):

> *But one thing I do, **forgetting those things which are behind** and reaching forward to those things which are ahead, I press toward the goal for the prize of the upward call of God in Christ Jesus* (Philippians 3:13-14).

> *Bless the Lord, O my soul, and **forget not all His benefits**: who forgives all your iniquities.... He has not dealt with us according to our sins, nor punished us according to our iniquities. For as the heavens are high above the earth, so great is His mercy toward those who fear Him; as far as the east is from the west, so far has He removed our transgressions from us* (Psalm 103:2-3;10-12).

Like Paul, you are supposed to forget the past, but remember the benefits of the Lord, particularly the fact that He has forgiven all of your sin. To forget your sin successfully, you must fill your mind with the reality of being forgiven.

Do it regularly. Let it become one of those things that you recite in your litany of praises to the One who saved you. Remember, whatever you focus on will become your reality.

You remember in order to forget.

Points to Ponder

1. Take a moment to remember and list some of the benefits of God in your life. Realizing that they are always embedded in testimonies—the stories of what God has done in you and for you—you will be remembering stories of the times He has demonstrated His goodness to you.

2. How can you tell when you are forgetting your sins—or forgetting your new reality? How do you feel in each case? How long does it take you to "get it"? As you grow in Christ, are you remembering His benefits more often and more quickly?

Meditation

Discussing conversion and salvation may seem too elementary. After all, by now shouldn't you have moved on to things that are deeper and grander?

Maybe not. This is your foundation in Christ. Make sure that everything you are thinking and doing is firmly based on it. This defines who you are, what you do, whom you listen to, where you go, and much more.

Sink into it; don't skip over it.

Chapter 7

Joy
Beni Johnson

AS THE PEOPLE OF God, we are supposed to bring Heaven to earth, and *joy* is a very big part of Heaven. Heaven is filled with it. Our responsibility is to bring that joy to earth.

Heaven has no depression in it, so we have no legal right to be depressed. If you are depressed, you need to recheck your life. Figure out why, and for Heaven and earth's sake, take care of it. The world needs to see happy, joyful, alive people of God who love and serve out of joy.

You might be thinking, "But what about all the horrible stuff that is going on in the world? Shouldn't that affect me?" Yes, it should. I met with a woman in our church who wanted to let me know some things that were going on in our city regarding the occult. After we met, I headed right over to our prayer house. I was feeling a little heavy and I needed to get God's perception on all that I had heard. As I walked and prayed in the prayer garden, I had a vision. In the vision, I was in a familiar place with Jesus. We were walking and holding hands, similar to the way that two best girlfriends would hold hands, shoulder to shoulder. It felt as though we were sharing intimate secrets. I was talking to Him about the information I had just received. I looked over at His other hand, which was closed. I could tell that He was holding something in secret in that hand. I asked Him what He had in His hand, and He opened it. I saw that He was holding the whole world. It looked so small. When I saw that, every bit of the heaviness left, and I realized that He has everything under His control and in His hand. Now that doesn't mean that I don't continue to pray over these matters for my city. But it does mean that I can't carry the heaviness. Jesus already did that; He carried it all to the cross.

What that means is that we can now fight *from* victory and not *for* victory. When Jesus said, "It is finished," can you imagine what happened in the demonic realm? I can see them saying, "Yeah, it's finished, and we won," only to be shocked in three days when Jesus overcame death. Yes, it was finished for the demons of hell. They had to go back to the drawing board and formulate a whole new plan. But in Heaven, they knew what Jesus meant. Everything was complete now—all that Jesus had set out to accomplish on earth.

He had set the captives free, healed the sick, raised the dead, and cast out demons (see Luke 4:18). He had died on the cross and then He rose from the dead. We need to become fully confident about what Jesus did, so we can become releasers of His victory here on earth.

I'm not saying that there won't be times when we have to pray with a burden. We might need to carry heavy burdens in times of prayer, but I do not believe we are allowed to carry them outside of our intercessions. He gives us an exchange program. We give Him our heavy burdens; He gives us rest—and joy.

The world is full of suffering. Jesus suffered. But while He lived on this earth, He knew how to live out of joy, even in the midst of suffering. He knew where His strength was. He had experienced the great joy of Heaven where there are no tears or sorrows.

The Bible tells us that we will enter into the joy of the Lord one day (see Matt. 25:21). If we feed ourselves with the joy of what God is doing here on earth, we will live as Jesus lived on earth. But if we feed ourselves with bad news all the time, we will live out of fear and despair.

The word "joy" is used 182 times in the Bible. This should remind us of the importance of being the joyful people we were created to be. We represent (or re-present) our heavenly Father to the world we live in. He is joyful. He laughs. He wants us to enter into His joy:

I have said these things to you so that My joy may be in you, and that your joy may be complete (John 15:11).

For you shall go out in joy, and be led back in peace; the mountains and the hills before you shall burst into song, and all the trees of the field shall clap their hands (Isaiah 55:12).

The Lord, your God, is in your midst, a warrior who gives victory; He will rejoice over you with gladness, He will renew you in His love; He will exult over you with loud singing (Zephaniah 3:17).

The joy of the Lord is your strength (Nehemiah 8:10).

Your sorrow will be turned into joy (John 16:20).

Looking to Jesus the pioneer and perfecter of our faith, who for the sake of tje joy that was set before Him endured the cross...(Hebrews 12:2).

Until now you have asked nothing in My name. Ask, and you will receive, that your joy may be full (John 16:24).

Serve the Lord with gladness; Come before His presence with singing (Psalm 100:2).

Let the righteous be glad; Let them rejoice before God; Yes, let them rejoice exceedingly (Psalm 68:3).

Your word was to me the joy and rejoicing of my heart; For I am called by Your name, O Lord God of hosts (Jeremiah 15:16).

And the disciples were filled with joy and with the Holy Spirit (Acts 13:52).

For the kingdom of God is not eating and drinking, but righteousness and peace and joy in the Holy Spirit (Romans 14:17).

You will find such verses about joy everywhere in the Bible. Read them in different translations—for your enjoyment.

Points to Ponder

1. Are you a naturally joyful person? How can you "graduate" from natural joy to the joy of the Lord? Are you naturally melancholy or subdued? What does the joy of the Lord look like when you express it?

    ....

    ....

    ....

2. Must joy be always exuberant? How can joy be synonymous with rest?

    ....

    ....

    ....

3. In your present season of life, what word about joy from the Bible captures you? Read it in several translations and memorize the one that best ministers to your spirit.

    ....

    ....

    ....

Meditation

Just now, when you read about joy, did your heart leap up, rejoicing? Or did you want to turn the page? Where did the word find you? In other words, where does the Word Himself find you right now?

Pour out your heart to Him (see Ps. 62:8). Tell Him what is on your heart, whether it is a heavy burden or a confession of delight in your current experience of His Kingdom. Ask Him to enable you to enter into the joy of your Master. He will answer that prayer.

Chapter 8

TRANSFORMED BY PROMOTION
BILL JOHNSON

TOWARD THE END OF His earthly life, Jesus gave His disciples the ultimate promotion. He told them that He no longer called them servants, but friends. To be in the same room with Him would have been more than they could have asked for. But Jesus had brought them into His life. They had proven themselves worthy of the greatest promotion ever experienced by human beings:

> *No longer do I call you servants, for a servant does not know what his master is doing; but I have called you friends, for all things that I heard from My Father I have made known to you* (John 15:15).

With this promotion, the disciples' attention would now shift from the task at hand to the One within reach. They had been given access to the secrets of the heart of God.

Servants do not know what their master is doing. They do not have access to the personal, intimate realm of their master. They are task-oriented. Obedience is their primary focus—and rightly so, for their lives depend on success in that area.

But friends have a different focus. It almost sounds blasphemous to say that obedience is not the top concern for the friend, but it is true. Obedience will always be important, as the previous verse highlights, *"You are my friends if you do whatever I command you"* (John 15:14). But friends are less concerned about disobeying than they are about disappointing. The focus of the disciples shifted from obeying the commandments to relating to the One who gives them. Instead of asking, "What should I do for Him?" now they wonder, "How do my choices affect Him?"

Several paradigm shifts happen in our hearts as we embrace this promotion. First, *what we know* changes, as we gain access to the heart of the Father. We gain freedom from knowing His heart.

Second, our *experience* changes. His heartbeat becomes our heartbeat, and we celebrate the shift in our desires. Divine encounters become our greatest memories, and personal transformation is the only possible result.

Third, our *function* in life changes radically. Instead of working *for* Him, we work *with* Him. We work not *for* His favor but *from* His favor. He entrusts us with more of His power, and we are naturally changed into His likeness more and more.

Fourth, our *identity* is transformed radically. Christians who live out of who they really are cannot be crippled by the opinions of others. They no longer work to fit into other people's expectations; they burn with the realization of who the Father says they are.

The classic example of the difference between servant and friends is found in the story of Mary and Martha. Mary chose to sit at Jesus' feet while Martha chose to work in the kitchen (see Luke 10:38-42). It was as though Martha was making sandwiches that Jesus had never ordered while Mary was enjoying Jesus' favor and using the time simply to be with Him. Mary wasn't a nonworker; she had learned to serve from His presence—only making the sandwiches that Jesus had ordered.

We usually think of the will of God as something fixed and unchangeable. We don't remember that we have a part to play. God told Moses to get out of the way when He was about to kill the wayward people that

Moses had led out of Egypt. Moses then reminded God that they weren't his people—they were God's. Not only that, he didn't lead them out of Egypt, God did! God acknowledged that he was right, and then He promised not to kill them after all.

The astonishing thing is not so much that God changed His mind and spared Israel. Rather, it was that He expected Moses to come into the counsel of His will, and Moses knew it. Abraham was another who understood this. These covenant friends throughout history seemed to have a common awareness of God's expectation that they should be involved in the demonstration of His will, even influencing the outcome of the matter. They understood that the responsibility rested on their shoulders, that they must act before God to get what people needed. God's will is not always focused on events; it is focused on His friends drawing near and coming into His presence, standing in their roles as delegated ones.

As a kid, you may have dreamed about being granted one wish. Solomon got one, and his opportunity forever raised the bar of our expectations in prayer. The disciples were given the same "wish," only better. Instead of one blank check, they were given an unlimited supply of blank checks, and this gift was specifically granted in the context of their friendship with God.

Along with their promotion to friendship, Jesus gave His disciples an amazing list of promises. Each promise was a blank check that they could use throughout their lives for the expansion of the Kingdom. Here they are, with special emphasis added:

> *If you abide in Me, and My words abide in you, you will ask **what you desire**, and it shall be done for you* (John 15:7).

> *You did not choose Me, but I chose you and appointed you that you should go and bear fruit, and that your fruit should remain, that **whatever you ask** the Father in My name, He may give you* (John 15:16).

> ***If you ask anything*** *in My name, I will do it* (John 14:14).

*Most assuredly, I say to you, **whatever you ask the Father** in my name He will give you. Until now you have asked nothing in My name. **Ask, and you will receive,** that your joy may be full* (John 16:23-24).

God never intended believers to be like puppets on strings. He actually makes Himself vulnerable to the desires of His people. In fact, it can be said, "If it matters to you, it matters to Him." It's not because He needs us, but because He loves us.

Points to Ponder

1. In the story of Mary and Martha, which sister have you usually identified with most readily? How did reading this short chapter change your approach to the meaning and value of servanthood versus friendship?

    ....

    ....

    ....

2. As you have embraced your own promotion to friendship with God, what changes have you noticed in the following?

    what you know...

    in your experiences...

    in your function in life...

    in your idenitity...

3. What have you asked the Lord for lately? Do you believe you will receive it? Why or why not?

    ....

    ....

    ....

Meditation

Lean into the heart of God. Yes, you can hear His heartbeat—even if you have never heard it before. Review His invitation to the disciples to become His friends and then take His statement personally; He is including you, too.

Say to yourself, "I am a friend of God." Then say to Him, "You call me Your friend." Put your name into the blank: "_____, who is a friend of God." Let these words clear up your confusion. No longer are you a servant. You are His friend. He says so.

You will not have to prove anything. Just keep leaning.

Chapter 9

FRIENDS AND CO-LABORERS
BILL JOHNSON

SERVANTS ARE NOT CO-LABORERS with their masters; friends are. We don't have servants today, so it can be hard for us to understand, but imagine what it would be like to have people living in your household who served you and carried out your will. A servant would know certain things about you, such as your hobbies, what you like for dinner, and what time you want coffee in the morning. But a servant would not share personal times with you. He wouldn't comfort you in your down times; you would not invite the servants in to discuss family problems or business decisions.

God has elevated us from servants to friends. Our relationship goes beyond employer-employee interactions. He is willing for us to share in His unfolding creative work. It's not that He lacks for ideas; it's just that He enjoys our participation.

And as friends, He makes us co-laborers with Him (see 2 Cor. 6:1). The normal Christian life is a partnership between God and each one of us, played out in everyday living as we become a gate of Heaven, releasing the manifestation of God's reality for those around us.

Too many Christians have a one-dimensional perspective on this idea of co-laboring. They think it's a robotic interplay between themselves and God in which their will is dialed down to zero and His will completely overtakes their desires and thoughts. They see themselves as remote-control beings, totally under the direction of a God who sits in Heaven and works the master controls. But that is exactly the opposite of what the Bible says. In fact, our ideas and desires and dreams have a monumental influence on how God carries out His plan in this world. We are co-laborers, meaning that apart from Christ our work is not complete, and at the same time, amazingly, *His work on earth is not complete without us.* God looks to you and me as contributors to what He is doing, not as robots who carry out His ideas.

Many of us, myself included, have prayed prayers in the past such as, "Oh God, take over my will!" That is easily one of the stupidest prayers anyone can pray. It devalues our will, which is one of the greatest things God ever created. Your will is so valuable that He wouldn't violate it even at the cost of His own Son. Without an independent will, we become animated playthings, dolls, programmed toys. But with a free will, we become lovers of God and willing partners with Him. And when we co-labor with Him, our ideas can literally change the course of history.

The Bible shows us how co-laboring works. At the Creation, God let Adam name all of the animals (see Gen. 2:19). Names in those days were more than just cute labels given to distinguish the creatures from one another. Names indicated what kind of nature this creature would express. God created it all; Adam added his creative expression by giving the animals certain natures. That's co-laboring.

One of the most extraordinary examples of co-laboring was the building of the temple, which was one of the most significant events in the Bible. At the temple's dedication, David's son Solomon said,

> *Blessed be the Lord God of Israel, who spoke with His mouth to my father David, and with His hand has fulfilled it, saying, "Since the day that I brought My people Israel out of Egypt, I have chosen no*

city from any tribe of Israel in which to build a house, that My name might be there; but I chose David to be over My people Israel." Now it was in the heart of my father David to build a temple for the name of the Lord God of Israel (1 Kings 8:15-17).

God was saying, "I did not choose a city, I chose a man, and the temple was in the heart of the man." It's as if He said, "The temple was not my idea. *David* was my idea." Incredible! David's creativity and desires wrote history because God embraced them. This is absolutely foreign to most of our way of thinking. We wait for instructions and work hard to suppress our own ideas. We think anything we do for God must flow directly from the divine throne and be carried out to the letter, as if from a heavenly instruction booklet.

This is not to cancel out the fact that God has very specific plans and ideas that we have no chance of changing. It's to our benefit to leave those concrete issues alone. And what are they? You can only learn through your relationship with Him. For example, God told David that He had chosen him to be the king and would make his name great, but God hadn't asked David for a house, and David wasn't the guy who was going to build it—his son was (see 2 Sam. 7). He gives us Kingdom principles that set up our parameters. Then He says, "Come! Let's dream together and write the story of human history!"

Like many pastors, I have foolishly taught that if you delighted yourself in the Lord, He would change your desires by telling you what to desire. I misunderstood the biblical concept behind this passage: *"Delight yourself also in the Lord, and He shall give you the desires of your heart"* (Ps. 37:4). That verse literally means that God wants to be influenced by what you think and dream. He is after your desires. He is after intimacy with you. He opens Himself to the desires of His people.

He likes going back and forth with you, throwing out His idea and waiting for your response. Jesus even said, "Whomever you forgive, I forgive."

Jesus said to them again, "Peace to you! As the Father has sent Me, I also send you." And when He had said this, He breathed on them, and said to them, "Receive the Holy Spirit. If you forgive the sins of any, they are forgiven them; if you retain the sins of any, they are retained (John 20:21-23).

Co-laboring is a huge aspect of ministry that many of us simply do not understand, because true friendship with God is so foreign to us.

Points to Ponder

1. With your heavenly Father, do you feel more like a servant or like a co-laborer (friend)? Why?

    ....

    ....

    ....

2. Can you point to a time in your own life when you became a partner with God, when your desires influenced the outcome of a situation?

    ....

    ....

    ....

3. Think of something that you are dealing with right now, something you may have already brought to God in prayer. How can you move in the direction of co-laboring in this situation?

    ....

    ....

    ....

Meditation

As you consider your corner of the world, what do you desire? The one line, "on earth as it is in heaven" is your mandate. Where would you like the Kingdom to come?

Turn your desires into prayers. With your spirit (spirit to Spirit) feel out the corresponding desires of your Savior and Friend and Father. Discuss your thoughts about the desires of your heart. Get lost in your friendship with Him. See what moves Him, and allow what moves Him to set your course.

Know that if He cancels one of your ideas, it's only because He has a better one in mind. And He would much rather listen to you dream than to have you cower before Him asking for your next task.

Chapter 10

Just Do It!

Kevin Dedmon

O VER THE YEARS, I have heard many Christians demand pastors to give them "the meat of the Word." What they mean is that they want an insightful Bible study that will give them more knowledge. Obviously, we must learn the truths of Scripture, which requires a foundation of information. But information (knowledge) is not the "meat of the Word."

Jesus was clear on this point. He said, *"My food* [KJV: "meat"] *is to do the will of Him who sent Me, and to finish His work"* (John 4:34). He goes on in the next verse to exhort the disciples to open their eyes to see the fields that are ripe for harvest (see John 4:35). I want to suggest that doing God's will, eating the meat of the Word, is not listening to a Bible teacher, but going and doing what it says, especially as it relates to working in the harvest fields.

James sums up this point well in his epistle when he instructs, *"Be doers of the word, and not hearers only, deceiving yourselves"* (James 1:22). Only so much talk should be tolerated before someone jumps up and shouts, "Let's go do it!"

The hardest part is the *going*. We are afraid. Only some of us are natural risk takers. Most of us would rather bargain our way out of doing something that seems dangerous. We think, "Instead of *going*, why don't I start a prayer meeting at the church to pray for this? After all, prayer is powerful and effective—and a lot safer."

I believe that we need to decide ahead of time to take risks, to just go ahead and do the things we believe God has put before us. I was leading an outreach one day in a neighborhood near our church. We had split up into two teams, going to various locations at which we felt there would be "divine appointments." At the end of the allotted time, we were to rendezvous and then head back to the church together.

After waiting for ten minutes at the rendezvous point, we surmised that the other team had been caught up in a lengthy divine appointment, so I decided to send my other two teammates off to find them, while I would stay at the designated location in case they came back in the meantime.

As I was standing on the curb, waiting, I noticed a young man walking toward me on the sidewalk. As he approached, a thought popped into my mind: "Roger." *Is that a word of knowledge?* I thought. I heard it again: "Roger."

I decided to take a risk and test out this word of knowledge. As he began to pass me on the sidewalk, I said, with as much confidence as I could muster, "Excuse me, but is your name Roger?" I fully expected this to be his name, which would lead to an incredible divine appointment.

With a look of disdain, he jumped off the sidewalk and said, "Noooo!" as if I were trying to "pick him up," and he proceeded on down the street. Filled with embarrassment at having just come off as some sort of predator, I thought about chasing him down to explain, but immediately realized that would probably just make things worse. I thought, *At least I did not say that God had told me that his name was Roger; at least I did not defame Christianity. He just thought I was a kook.*

My next thought was, *Thanks a lot, God, I just made a fool of myself because I took a risk with a word of knowledge I thought you had given me.* The response I heard shocked me, "Kevin, I gave you the name 'Roger.'"

"What? You purposely gave me the wrong name?" I shot back.

"Yes, I did, because I wanted to see if you would continue to take risk even if you did not get the right information." He went on to say that He was not as interested in the success of the performance as He was in my courage to act, apart from the outcome.

I know this story is out of the box for many, and I would not want to suggest that God is in the habit of giving false words of knowledge to test our resolve. But it was a valuable lesson for me to realize that sometimes I will interpret inaccurately what I think He says and sometimes He might even "set me up," but that either way, He wants me to step out boldly in faith. It is always better to make some mistakes than to do nothing out of timidity.

We do not have to maintain 100 percent accuracy to avoid repercussions. Some people remember the Old Testament warnings and they are worried about being called a "false prophet." Jesus identified false prophets by the fruit of their character, not the accuracy of their words (see Matt. 7:15-20). Also, a false prophet can have a right word, which conversely implies that a true prophet can have a wrong word. Therefore, having a wrong word does not automatically make someone a false prophet. Paul instructed the Corinthians: *"Let two or three prophets speak, and let the others judge"* (1 Cor. 14:29). If the prophets were expected to be mistake-free, then there would be no need to "judge" the words.

Again, God is more interested in the level of risk we undertake with a pure heart to bless those around us than in our playing it safe with what we are absolutely sure of.

Misunderstanding the warnings about the Old Testament prophets, many have shied away from risk for fear of being "stoned" over a mistake. This applies to prophetic words, witnessing, and more. There is such fear in somehow failing in the encounters that God has set up for us that we tend to ignore the responsibility rather than take a risk. But without risk, there is no reward. *"Without faith it is impossible to please Him"* (Heb. 11:6).

Points to Ponder

1. Are you a natural risk taker? Whether you are a risk taker by nature or not—or an occasional risk taker—how do you respond to Kevin's encouragement to "just do it"?

    ....

    ....

    ....

2. What is the most "out of the box" thing God has ever asked you to do? How did you handle it?

    ....

    ....

    ....

Meditation

You know and believe the truth of this verse from the Psalms: *"Your word is a lamp to my feet, and a light to my path"* (Ps. 119:105). Consider the fact that God's Word—either as part of written Scripture or as His Spirit enlivens a word or phrase to your spirit—brings with it light for the steps ahead. Your job is not to worry about the details, but only to move your feet, one at a time, step by step.

Do you tend to hesitate on the threshold of doing His word?

Talk with Him about it. He has been waiting for an opportunity to have this conversation—for your benefit and for His. He is already turning the lights on for you.

Chapter 11

Light Therapy
Kevin Dedmon

Last ski season, I was paired up with a 30-year-old man to ride on the chair lift at a local ski area. On the way up to the top of the mountain, I noticed that he was wincing in apparent pain. He explained that a few days prior he had been bitten by a brown recluse spider twice, once on the left side of his chest, and the other on the back of his left shoulder. The bites had caused the muscles on the left side of his body to be somewhat paralyzed, while at the same time leaving him riddled with pain.

He had already taken one run down the mountain and found that he could barely ski because of the debilitating effects of the spider's venom. He had planned to go up one more time to see if he could work out the stiffness, but the pain had increased so much from the physical exertion of the first run that he was worried he might not be able to make it down the mountain the second time.

I asked what he had done to treat the symptoms. He told me that his wife had forced him to go to a "light therapist," who focused certain types of ultraviolet light on the inflamed areas. I asked, "How is that working out for you?" to which he replied, "Not too good!" He went on to explain that this "light therapist" was the only apparent hope he had to treat the pronounced symptoms, but that he had received several treatments without any noticeable change in his condition.

I casually mentioned that I had access to a more powerful light that could take care of his problems. That got his attention. He asked what kind of light I was speaking of. I responded, "It's the Light of the world, Jesus, and he can heal you right here, right now." He explained that he had never believed in Jesus, but agreed to let me pray for him as we were heading up the mountain on the chair lift.

So I simply released the light of the presence of Jesus Christ on him in a very short prayer, without touching him, and then asked him to tell me what he was experiencing. To his surprise, all of the pain had completely left his body.

He was so excited about the changes that had occurred that he began to ask questions about my belief in Christ. After I quickly answered a few questions, he expressed that he had always thought of Christianity as just another philosophy, not as a relationship with a living God. Briefly, I went on to explain that he too could have a relationship with Jesus, and that he could experience His presence any time he wanted. To that, he only responded that he was already feeling a presence all over him and that this was all very foreign to him.

Knowing I had only a short time remaining before our chair would reach the top of the mountain, I asked how the numbness in his muscles was doing. He stretched a little, and then he reported that there was still no change. Upon hearing this status report, I asked if he would like another session of the "Light therapy," to which he readily agreed.

Once again, I released God's presence in a simple, short prayer, and then I asked how he felt. With a shocked look on his face, he exclaimed that all of the numbness was gone. "But wait a minute," he said, "let me get off of the chair lift to check it out," as if I had used some kind of spell on him to make him temporarily *think* he was healed. Nevertheless, it was obvious that he was shaken by the encounter with God's presence surrounding the chair lift, which prompted more questions. I answered several of them and then blessed him as we disembarked from the lift.

I skied over to my wife and daughter, who had been in the chair in front of us, and began to help them with their snowboards. In the midst of our getting everything adjusted, the man skied over to inform me that all of the pain and numbness was now gone. He did not hurt anywhere anymore, and his left side felt the same as his right side now. He was so excited that he yelled out a big "Thank you!" and then skied off down the mountain as though he was in a race!

I'm sure that he had a lengthy conversation with his wife that evening about the other "Light therapist" he had encountered that day.

All I had to do was notice the need, and then take some risk to meet it with God's power. I suppose that many believers are intimidated by the idea of ministering in God's supernatural power, because they just do not feel as though they have the necessary ability to confidently release the Kingdom. I want to propose, however, that all believers possess the potential to operate in this way if they want to. Every believer has the potential ability to heal the sick, prophesy, and set people free. I know that too many of us are unaware that we are actually anointed beyond our ability as disciples of Jesus.

Jesus prayed to His Father about the disciples, saying, *"As You sent Me into the world, I also have sent them into the world"* (John 17:18). After the resurrection, Jesus informed the disciples, *"As the Father has sent Me, I also send you"* (John 20:21). We have been *sent* to do the same things that Jesus did—to proclaim freedom for the prisoners, recovery of sight for the blind, release for the oppressed, and the year of the Lord's favor (see Luke 4:18-19).

In other words, we are supposed to release the Kingdom wherever we go, to whomever we meet. That was His mission, and it is our mission as well.

Points to Ponder

1. Have you ever had any experiences like this one? If you have, what was it like? What did you learn from your experience that will help you next time? If you have not had such an experience, why not? Have you assumed that such experiences are for "other people"? What will help you step into the fullness of your calling as a disciple of Jesus?

    ....

    ....

    ....

2. How do you think God would like to use your individual combination of gifts, traits, and interests? Where does He want you to release His Kingdom?

    ....

    ....

    ....

Meditation

In your mind's eye, think about the places you went yesterday and today and the people you saw. Perhaps you are in a place with other people around you right now as you read this.

Ask the Holy Spirit to help you see with His eyes. He has put you wherever you go for a reason. See if you can identify His loving direction and if you can begin to release more of His Kingdom. Even if startling miracles do not result, you can at least bring His blessing to those you meet, and you can learn more about being His follower.

How can you prepare your expectations for tomorrow? If you take ownership for the needs around you, God will reveal Himself to those you touch in His name.

Chapter 12

LIVING UNDER THE INFLUENCE
BILL JOHNSON

THE PURPOSE OF GOD'S wondrous stories is to draw us into the passionate pursuit of more of His presence. His intention is to draw us to live under the influence of His presence rather than simply obeying His principles. He has called us to Himself through His kindness; it is the kindness of God that leads us to repentance. Experiencing complete forgiveness and having our minds renewed results in deep affection and intimacy. This is the bedrock for ongoing Kingdom experiences. The Kingdom of God and the presence of God are inseparable.

We have many spiritual gifts, but for the most part they remain embryonic in form. It's not that they have no present purpose or effect. They do. A person is as likely to see cancer healed in his or her first healing miracle as a simple headache. The smallest measure of faith can move a mountain. By embryonic, I simply mean that these gifts are alive, but they're small and not fully formed. The Lord wants us to fan them into flame and to become mature. Gifts are free, but maturity is expensive.

True as this is, there are moments when the gifts of God explode and come into great fruition through one simple act of boldness. In other words, what we thought would take years to grow sometimes grows in an instant. But the climate must be right—a climate of great faith and courage. This is what happened to the apostle Paul.

When Saul began serving Christ, he was the lesser-known sidekick of Barnabas, *"a good man, full of the Holy Spirit and faith"* (Acts 11:24). Luke identified the team as "Barnabas and Saul." But one day came when that changed.

An occultist named Elymas rose up against the pair to undermine the work of the Gospel and deceive potential converts. Boldness came upon Paul from the Holy Spirit:

> *But Elymas the sorcerer (for so his name is translated) withstood them, seeking to turn the proconsul away from the faith. Then Saul, who also is called Paul, filled with the Holy Spirit, looked intently at him and said, "O full of all deceit and all fraud, you son of the devil, you enemy of all righteousness, will you not cease perverting the straight ways of the Lord? And now, indeed, the hand of the Lord is upon you, and you shall be blind, not seeing the sun for a time." And immediately a dark mist fell on him, and he went around seeking someone to lead him by the hand* (Acts 13:8-11).

Through one act of boldness, Saul helped create the atmosphere for increase to be released over his life. Soon afterward, and from that point on, Luke mentioned the apostolic duo as "Paul and Barnabas."

Courage in the moment was all that was needed to unleash the potential that had been lying dormant in Paul. Boldness became the catalytic ingredient that released immediate promotion. Isn't it amazing how Paul drew from his own testimony for this manifestation of the Kingdom? He himself had received a rebuke from Jesus that resulted in short-term blindness. He'd seen that miracle and knew that God would do it again.

The gifts within us are waiting for a shift to take place in our hearts. This happens when the internal world of our spirit rises to meet the challenge of the external world. In a way, it means that every believer is a leader.

Not every person has a position with a leadership title, but all lead. In fact, the day is coming when the nations of the world will stream to the people of God to hear what God is saying (see Mic. 4:2 and Isa. 2:2-3).

Jesus taught us that it should be natural for all believers to know His voice, so it should be equally natural to be able to tell others what He is saying. The author of Hebrews affirmed the leadership assignment for all Christians when he said, *"By this time you ought to be teachers"* (Heb. 5:12). The same Holy Spirit has been given to every believer, making it possible for every believer to have a significant role in bringing transformation to individuals, cities, and nations.

There will always be generals in the army. But a private in the New Testament army has access to more authority than any of the generals of the Old Testament army did. Jesus made the point by saying that *"he who is least in the kingdom of heaven is greater than he* [John] *"* (Matt. 11:11).

When each one of us recognizes that he or she has this kind of influence, it shifts our priorities and changes how we learn, what we think we need to learn, and how we handle the challenges that come our way.

It is interesting to note, however, that the greatest responsibility for us as leaders has nothing to do with leading. It has to do with following. I am designed to live under the influence of the King and His Kingdom, and I must make sure the right things make an impact on me so that my impact on the world around me is what God intends.

Witnessing supernatural wonders produces a pronounced influence on a person's soul and spirit. The result is wonderful; it draws them to the One who does wonders. Conversely, when the supernatural interventions of God are absent or rare, people tend to fall away from God. Look what happened to Israel. (See Judges 2:7,10,12; Joshua 24:31.) Exposure to the supernatural works of God changes the capacity of leaders to lead, thereby changing the bent of the people of God to pursue Him.

Such exposure is the equivalent of a spiritual change of DNA. The people of God inherit a heart for God through the leader's influence. Leaders create an atmosphere, either good or bad. True spiritual leaders are those who carry their own Heaven-centered spiritual weather system that permeates their realm of influence and authority.

Points to Ponder

1. Do you consider yourself a leader? Why or why not? Has this brief chapter given you a new perspective? What can you do differently?

    ....

    ....

    ....

2. What does it mean to say, "Gifts are free, but maturity is expensive?"

    ....

    ....

    ....

3. Who has "sown into" your life? Whom are you sowing into? Whom are you influencing with the Heaven that you carry, and how is that influence being expressed?

    ....

    ....

    ....

Meditation

You will be strongly influenced by your firsthand experience of God's authority as expressed through others, for better or for worse. In the absence of supernatural experiences of God during the long wilderness years of Israel's wanderings, an entire generation grew up with no compass. They had only heard about the God of wonders, so they rebelled.

Reducing Christianity to what is humanly possible is responsible for the cold-hearted condition of many generations throughout history. Moral teaching, while absolutely necessary, seldom lights a fire in the hearts of people who may have to "take a bullet" for an eternal purpose.

The Church you belong to was never meant to be known for its disciplines. You and your fellow believers are meant to be known for your passions and for the Heaven you bring to earth.

Chapter 13

CALLING FORTH HIS DESIRES

BENI JOHNSON

WHEN ANY OF US go into God's presence and tap into the realm of Heaven, we position ourselves to receive great breakthroughs. In such times, I often see faces, places, and situations in my mind's eye. I often feel as if God is showing me things that I need to think about and brood over in the way that a mother hen broods over her eggs. Genesis 1:1-2 says, *"The earth was without form, and void; and darkness was on the face of the deep. And the Spirit of God was hovering over the face of the waters."* He was brooding over the earth to bring His will into being.

To be honest, most of the time I don't brood; I just agree. I agree with the plans that God already has for people's lives, for regions, and for the earth. "Yes God, do that." "Go there, Father." "Thank you, Holy Spirit." When I pray this way, I feel as though I am praying from His heart and calling into existence the very desires that are already in the heart of God.

One of the things we need to be careful about is going before God with our own agendas. If we go before God and already have an idea of what we want God to do, we close ourselves off from receiving from and partnering with God in what He may want to do in the moment. In fact, God may want to do something completely different. It is almost as if we handcuff God.

Often, when people ask me to pray for them, they come with an agenda or an idea of what they want to ask God to do. Sometimes their requests are not on God's agenda for the moment. We need to learn how to be sensitive and move with the Holy Spirit. We need to listen to the heartbeat of God and not always present our ideas to Him as if they are demands. It's not about whether agendas are wrong or right, but it's about spending time with God and resting in His presence.

The amazing thing to me is that God is waiting for us to enter into Him. He is longing for us to see His world, to see into that glorious realm of His Kingdom. He wants us to partner with Him for heavenly breakthrough. God's *yes* together with our *yes* is what brings about breakthrough in prayer.

I am continually amazed that God would choose to partner with us. But at the same time, it makes all the sense in the world that He would want us to join with Him in making history. We are, after all, His children. He is a great and all-powerful God and also a loving and caring Father who, incredibly, wants to be involved in our lives and wants us to be involved in His Kingdom. He wants us to help build His Kingdom here on earth.

Some of our prophetic acts come straight from the Lord. But I think that some of the things that we do are good ideas that the Father approves of. First Kings chapter 8 says that God chose David and that it was in David's heart to build a house for the Lord (see 1 Kings 8:16-17). God told David in verse 18, *"Whereas it was in your heart to build a temple for My name, you did well that it was in your heart."* God chose a man that He knew would say *yes* and God said *yes* to David's ideas. Everything else is history.

When our daughter Leah was expecting her first baby, she asked, with permission from her husband, if I could be her childbirth coach. I had had three children by natural birth, and she told me, "You're the pro, Mom." It was an honor for me.

God is always breaking into our natural world and showing us the spirit realm. That's what happened in this birthing experience with my daughter. In a natural birth, you can invite friends and family into the labor room. Our daughter is a very social being and loved having those friends and family visit up until the time of the birth. As you may know, toward the end of the labor, there is a time that is the most intense. It takes all of your concentration just to make it through the contractions. Whenever a contraction would start, we would release peace over Leah, and then all of her focus was on me to listen to my instructions.

One of our friends came into the room at one of those moments and began talking, not really paying attention to the intensity of what was happening. But Leah seemed to be OK with it. After the delivery, I asked her about the distractions in the room. She told me that she really didn't notice because she was so focused on my voice and what I was telling her to do. As she told me that, I had a revelation about intercession. When God gives us strategies to pray, we can become so focused on His voice that we don't get distracted. Nothing can take us away from His voice. There were times during delivery that my daughter and I would lock eyes as well. She drew strength from looking into my eyes. There was an intensity or determination in my eyes that she picked up on, and it kept her going.

There are times in our lives when we must stay that close to God, locking onto His words and His vision. We can be sure that when God gives us ideas and strategies and we look to Him for understanding on how to pray for them, then the birthing or breakthrough will come. When we are focused on Him to that degree, all we have to do is agree with God and partner with the things that are already on His heart. No agenda required.

Points to Ponder

1. Think about your own intercessory prayer. Do you feel you have "partnered" with God at times? What have you learned about focusing on Him?

    ....

    ....

    ....

2. What is the difference between bringing God your own prepared agenda versus bringing Him one of your own ideas that He welcomes?

    ....

    ....

    ....

3. In what ways have you seen results from agreeing with God's agenda?

    ....

    ....

    ....

Meditation

Quiet your heart and mind so that you can draw near to God. For the sake of effective prayer, see if you can detect his "heartbeat." If you can do it, pray along with the intentions of His heart. If you cannot, talk to Him about it. Ask Him to be your "coach." Ask Him to show you how to focus on Him, and how to eliminate distractions from your attention.

You are not concentrating so much on the results as you are on Him. His answers to your prayers will always be perfect and far better than you could specify from your own limited perspective.

God's *yes* to you and your *yes* to Him are all that are needed.

Chapter 14

God Is Always Speaking
Kris Vallotton

THE LORD IS MORE determined and excited to speak to us than we are to hear from Him. We must realize that God is always speaking but that He is *not human* and His first language is *not English*! If we can grasp this revelation and realize that most of us do not really know how well we see and hear God, we can begin to "tune our receivers to His station."

No matter where you are at the moment, there is music playing all around you (even if you cannot hear any). By simply turning on a radio, you would pick up the music that has been there the whole time. Your body and ears were never designed to perceive radio waves.

Likewise, God's voice is always around you; you just need to learn to "tune in" to His wavelength. To do that, you need the gift of prophecy, which will equip you to tap into the spirit realm that surrounds you even though you can't hear it with your naked ear. The gift of prophecy is like a radio receiver from Heaven. It gives you the ability to hear what God has been speaking to you all along but you were unable to perceive before you knew about this gift.

Most of us struggle to hear the voice of God, because the enemy does not want us to hear Him. Jesus explained what happens so often when God speaks, but we doubt what we hear:

The sower sows the word. And these are the ones by the wayside where the word is sown. When they hear, Satan comes immediately and takes away the word that was sown in their hearts (Mark 4:14-15).

Satan's objective is to prevent us from receiving or transmitting God's comfort and encouragement to one another through the prophetic word. He comes along and tries to convince us that we did not hear God clearly or that it was not God's voice at all. If the enemy can persuade us that the word spoken to us was not really God, then he is able to rob us of the benefits of that word. If he can convince us not to speak the word of the Lord by making us feel foolish, or convince us that it was just our imagination and not a prophetic word, than he has succeeded in stealing the fruit of God's word in someone else's life.

As we are learning to tune into the voice of the Holy Spirit, we must realize that not every voice that speaks to us from the spirit realm is from God. John wrote this advice: *"Beloved, do not believe every spirit, but test the spirits, whether they are of God; because many false prophets have gone out into the world"* (1 John 4:1). This passage makes it clear that we (the beloved) are quite able to hear from spirits other than the Holy Spirit and we need to be careful not to listen to the wrong spirit and thereby become false prophets.

Practice makes perfect. With experience, each one of us can learn to distinguish between the four possible sources of spiritual input:

1. Your own spirit. Each of us is a spirit that has a soul and a body. When you are born again, your spirit comes to life, making it possible to hear from the spirit realm—like your "receiver"—but it can generate its own "signals" as well.

2. The Holy Spirit. You want to hear His voice, even if He is very quiet sometimes.

3. Evil spirits. Spirits from the evil realm can speak to Christians just as they spoke to Jesus when He encountered the devil in the wilderness.

4. Angels. According to Hebrews 1, these are spirits who are sent to render service to the saints. They can speak to you about the things of God.

You will gain experience as you step out in faith, trying to listen to the Holy Spirit. You cannot grow in the gifts of the Spirit without making mistakes.

The Bible says, *"He who receives a prophet in the name of a prophet shall receive a prophet's reward"* (Matt. 10:41). What is a prophet's reward? The ability to *see* and *hear* the word. Everyone who values Jesus as prophet and receives the words that He speaks received the ability to see and hear. A grace is released with His words that opens eyes and ears.

Valuing the word of the Lord means that we make time to hear Him. Moses walked past the burning bush in the desert and heard nothing until he stopped and turned aside (see Exod. 3:2-4). In the same way, we need to set aside time to diligently seek God in order to hear Him.

> *But from there you will seek the Lord your God, and you will find Him if you seek Him with all your heart and with all your soul* (Deuteronomy 4:29).

> *For the eyes of the Lord run to and fro throughout the whole earth, to show Himself strong on behalf of those whose heart is loyal to Him* (2 Chronicles 16:9).

Even if God should speak audibly from Heaven, some people would only hear it as the sound of thunder (see John 12:28-29). The difference between being deaf and not deaf is not how loudly God speaks, but how open we are to hearing Him speak.

Jesus said, *"My sheep hear My voice, and I know them, and they follow Me"* (John 10:27). Moses said, *"Oh, that all the Lord's people were prophets and that the Lord would put His Spirit upon them!"* (Num. 11:29). Knowledge is power. God does not want the prideful to be the powerful ones in His Kingdom. Therefore, He hides His word so that only the hungry and the humble have access to His voice. (See Luke 10:21.)

Prophecy, in its simplest form, is merely hearing from the Holy Spirit and repeating what He has said.

Points to Ponder

1. See if you can give examples from your own life of hearing (1) the voice of your own spirit, (2) the voice of an evil spirit, (3) the voice of an angel, (4) the voice of the Holy Spirit. How could you tell the difference between the sources of what you heard?

    ....

    ....

    ....

2. List some of the reasons you sometimes do not hear God's voice. What can you do about them?

    ....

    ....

    ....

3. What is the most common way in which God speaks to you personally?

    ....

    ....

    ....

....

Meditation

Cultivating a pure heart is vitally important in communicating with God. Only the pure in heart will see God. *"Blessed are the pure in heart, For they shall see God"* (Matt. 5:8).

Take some time to ask the Lord to search your heart. Allow Him to cultivate the soil, so that the seeds of His words will have a place to grow. With humility and spiritual hunger as your guide, give Him more of your trust.

Chapter 15

Character—With Power
Bill Johnson

Many believers have made it their primary goal in life to be well-respected citizens of their communities. Good character enables us to be solid contributors to society, but most of what is recognized as a Christian lifestyle can be accomplished by people who don't even know God.

Every believer should be highly respected—*and more.* While good character must be at the heart of anything we do, we will continue to be recognized by the world merely as nice people—until the Church returns to Jesus' model for Kingdom living.

Some Christians consider it more noble to choose character over spiritual power. But we must not separate the two. In fact, it is unjustifiable and illegitimate to do so. Only when taken together do character and power allow for the key response, which is obedience.

Once, while teaching a group of students about the importance of signs and wonders in the ministry of the gospel, a young man spoke up, saying, "I'll pursue signs and wonders when I know I have more of the character of Christ in me." As good as that may sound, it comes from a religious mind-set, not a heart that is abandoned to the gospel of Jesus Christ. In response to the student's comment, I opened my Bible and read the Lord's charge to His disciples:

All authority has been given to Me in heaven and on earth. Go there-fore and make disciples of all the nations, baptizing them in the name of the Father and of the Son and of the Holy Spirit, teaching them to observe all things that I have commanded you; and lo, I am with you always, even to the end of the age (Mattew 28:18-20).

Then I asked him, "Who gave you the right to determine when you are ready to obey His command?"

Character is shaped through obedience. Obedience is doing what Je-sus has told us to do. Jesus commanded His disciples to go and teach the things He had taught them, and part of what He had taught them was how to do signs and wonders. He had commanded them to *"Heal the sick, cleanse the lepers, raise the dead, cast out demons. Freely you have re-ceived, freely give"* (Matt. 10:8). Part of godly character is obedience to Je-sus' commands—all of them.

Is it possible that the reason we see so few miracles in North Amer-ica is because too many people have thought they had to become better Christians before God could use them? Yes! That single lie has kept us in perpetual immaturity, because it protects us from the power-encounters that would transform us. We take our converts and we train and train them until they have no life, vision, or ingenuity left. Instead, we should be teaching them to walk in their identity as world-changers, people who can find multiple opportunities to serve because of their character, pas-sion, and spiritual power.

Both the Old and New Testaments are filled with great examples of people who were empowered and anointed for supernatural endeav-ors. Not always did those people manifest mature character traits, but they became all that God wanted them to be. King Saul is a good ex-ample. God spoke, saying that the Spirit of the Lord would come upon him and turn him into *"another man"* (see 1 Sam. 10:6). Then *"God gave him another heart"* (verse 9), and he *"prophesied among the proph-ets"* (verse 11).

I have a dear friend who had a huge character flaw that spiritually crip-pled him and his family for a season. Yet during this time, he still had a very strong prophetic anointing. He was not the first person to think that his successful ministry was a sign of God's approval of his private life.

I felt a keen sense of responsibility to bring him under discipline for the sake of his church, my church, and the places he ministered. I confronted him with his secret sin, and he wept with deep sorrow. He accepted my direction as necessary when I told him to stop giving prophetic words for a season. But after several months, the story of Saul kept coming to mind, and it troubled me. I realized that if I didn't allow my friend to minister under the anointing God had given him, I would be limiting his exposure to the very thing that would seal and establish his victory over sin.

When I released him to prophesy again, there was a new purity and power in his voice. His personal encounter with the anointing in ministry "turned him into another man."

Make no mistake, character is a supreme issue with God. But His approach is much different from ours. His righteousness and character cannot be built into us by our own efforts. It can only be developed when we quit striving and learn to abandon ourselves completely to His will. Like the disciples, we need to wait for the "power from on High" to come, but when it does, we need to spread it abroad, not bury it.

Why are we so afraid of error and so leery of experiencing God? Of course many deceived groups have come from those who based their beliefs on experiences that were in conflict with Scripture. But that should not drive us into the doctrinally stable camps that are powerless. We don't want to bury our gifts and tell the Master when He comes that we were afraid of being wrong (see Matt. 25).

At the cross, sin and its nature were yanked out by the roots. It's been finished off. Instead of calling out to God for more power to live in victory, I could be asking for power and boldness to obey His commands and do miracles. We need to make sure that we are not camping on the wrong side of the cross.

Power and character are so closely aligned in Scripture that you cannot be weak in one without undermining the other.

Points to Ponder

1. What part of this brief chapter jumped out at you as having a personal application? How does it affect your assumptions?

    ....

    ....

    ....

2. Do you know someone who displays both good character and powerful spiritual gifts? What did that person used to be like years ago, and how did he or she grow to be more like Jesus?

    ....

    ....

    ....

3. For the most part, which side of the cross are you "camping" on?

    ....

    ....

    ....

Meditation

Your relationship with the Holy Spirit will ensure that your character and your spiritual power walk hand-in-hand. The command, *"Do not grieve the Holy Spirit"* (Eph. 4:30) is character-centered. When you depart from the character of Christ by sinning—doing wrong things or failing to do right things—you bring grief to the Holy Spirit. The command, *"Do not quench the Spirit"* (1 Thess. 5:19) concerns obedience to His leading. To quench means to stop the flow of His power.

Reflect on times you may have justified your decisions and actions in ways that either quenched or grieved God's Spirit. Turn to Him in prayer, and tell Him what you want to do from now on.

Chapter 16

KINGDOM INCREASE

BANNING LIEBSCHER

SIGNS, WONDERS, HEALINGS, AND prophecy are being restored once again to the Church, becoming consistently demonstrated not just in crusades, but in everyday life both inside and outside church walls. It's not only happening through the hands of those in professional ministry. Soccer moms, businesspeople, teachers, children, and many others are witnessing the Word being made manifest in their regular lives.

For years, we primarily heard these kinds of testimonies from missionaries and itinerant preachers and we rejoiced with them. But now it's no longer only stories from third-world countries; the full Gospel of the Kingdom is being preached with signs and wonders in the nations of the West.

If the worldwide awakening and Kingdom increase happening right now were to end today, it would still go down in the history books as the most extensive and accelerated revival of all time. Yet what is the most exciting is that we are only at the beginning stages of what God purposes to do! He is intent on giving His Son what He asked for: the nations of the earth as His inheritance (see Ps. 2:8). God is setting us up for something extraordinary. A new breed of revivalist is emerging—those who burn with holy passion and who will listen to their Father's heartbeat and respond to His desires.

As a youth pastor, I had the opportunity to speak in Christian clubs on high school campuses. Many times I found that the Christian students were just trying to survive in the midst of a worldly generation. They huddled together, trying to strengthen themselves so they wouldn't fall away. I imagined them gathering each week and saying, "OK, we made it through one more week, but just barely. Whew! It's bad out there. People are smoking, doing drugs, having sex, and using the Lord's name in vain." Then they would turn to one another and ask, "Are you still saved?" "Yeah, are you still saved?" "Yeah." "OK. Good. Let's meet back here next week to make sure we're still saved."

That's not what anybody really said, but I know that was what was going on under the surface, because they had such a survival mentality. They were so shaken by their environment that they couldn't dream of fulfilling the Great Commission. They didn't realize that they had the supernatural power to win the entire campus with the Gospel.

But the mind-set is shifting, at all age levels. People are learning and becoming engaged in the pursuit of seeing God's glory cover the earth. No longer satisfied to simply survive in the kingdom of the world, they want to see it transformed into the Kingdom of our God (see Rev. 22:15).

It is not too much to say that we are called to take over the world. We are part of a revolution. We have been appointed to overthrow the government of darkness that has enslaved people in sin and sickness and to establish the Kingdom of Light on the earth as it is in Heaven. This revolution is not an anarchy of violence and control; it is a heavenly reformation, where truth spoken and love is demonstrated with supernatural power.

In 1975, Bill Bright and Loren Cunningham had similar visions from the Lord. One of them saw seven "mountains" and the other saw seven "mind molders" (spheres of influence) in society.[1] Lance Wallnau has carried the Seven Mountains message into the present day. Whoever commands and controls these mountains and spheres of influence sets the agenda and atmosphere in a society. God wants us to control them with Kingdom wisdom, love, joy, and power:

- Family

- Religion

- Economy

- Education

- Government

- Arts and media

- Science and technology

The new breed of revivalist emerging in the earth today will not only stand behind pulpits, but also will step into every realm of society to heal and deliver, turning the nations of the earth from being cursed to being healed and blessed. God wants to take hold of *all* believers (the salt of the earth—see Matt. 5:13) and throw them out into the far reaches of the nations.

Some of the new revivalists are CEOs of multibillion-dollar companies. Others are women who start up homes for unwed mothers, or social workers who change the way we take care of our children, politicians who make laws that reflect the counsel of the Lord, judges who extend the scepter of God's justice in the earth, authors who write books that reveal the character of God to a nation, screenwriters who create movies that compel us to action for the good, and school principals who uncover better methods to educate students.

I know people who are revivalists in different positions in society. One is the superintendent of a school district in California. Another is an Olympic and X Games gold medalist. Another is the lead singer of a rock band. Another is a lawyer in the military. Another is a businessman who has started a large orphanage and school.

These people are doing what they love to do, *and* they are being used by God. They are the salt of the earth. The convergence of their individual abilities and passions with God's call on their lives has made them "salty."

Like them, you and I can offer our yearnings and inclinations to God, seeking his anointing with Heaven's fire and purpose. As He helps us identify the dreams in our hearts and equips us with strength and power, we will be able to bring change and healing in society, further fulfilling Jesus' Great Commission to *"Go therefore and make disciples of all the nations, baptizing them in the name of the Father and of the Son and of the Holy Spirit, teaching them to observe all things that I have commanded you"* (Matt. 28:19-20). Far from being mindless servants who care only about reading the Bible and going to church, we have been called to partner with Heaven.

Endnote

1. See transcript of interview with Loren Cunningham on the original Seven Mountains Vision: "7 Spheres" (Nov. 19, 2007), http://www.reclaim7mountains.com/apps/articles/default.asp?articleid=40087&columnid=4347

Points to Ponder

1. Is the Great Commission meant only for special disciples who are passionate about evangelism? Why or why not?

   ....

   ....

   ....

2. In which of the seven mountains of influence do you find yourself? How has God called you to spread the Kingdom there?

   ....

   ....

   ....

....

Meditation

When you meet with the Lord in prayer, where do the thoughts of your heart take you? As many times as you may have had to seek His restorative strength after a day or a week on the battlefield, how has He provided you with new vision and resolve? Are you relying on Him only for survival strength—or also for revival strength?

Today when you meet with Him, take stock of your life. Look at it in terms of how "salty" you are. Evaluate where He has positioned you and ask Him to shed His light on the next steps of your future path.

Chapter 17

PRAYING IN THE SPIRIT
BILL JOHNSON

WHEN WE STRENGTHEN OURSELVES in the Lord, we focus on bringing our hearts, minds, and bodies in line with the purposes of God. This results in our having the strength to be true to that purpose in the face of difficulty and opposition. For the most part, we are not doing the building. God is doing the building, as are the men and women He has commissioned to disciple His body.

For example, Paul described himself as a "master builder" who laid the spiritual foundations of the house of God, the community of the redeemed, in Corinth (see 1 Cor. 3:10). A little later in the same epistle, he also thanked God that *"I speak with tongues more than you all"* (1 Cor. 14:18). Speaking in tongues, or praying in the Spirit, was something that Paul did to keep himself strong as a Kingdom-builder.

Jude writes about it as well: *"But you, beloved, building yourselves up on your most holy faith, praying in the Holy Spirit"* (Jude 1:20). Paul again expressed this idea of building yourself up by praying in the Spirit when he wrote to the Corinthians: *"He who speaks in a tongue edifies himself"* (1 Cor. 14:4). The word "edify" means "build up." When we pray in tongues, we are building something. Lance Wallnau calls it an internal edifice (from the same root as "edify") of faith from which the purposes of God become manifest.

How does praying in tongues accomplish this? When we speak in tongues, we are using our voices to give utterance to the expressions of our spirits as they commune with the Holy Spirit. This is powerful because our spirits are praying in perfect agreement with God. By engaging our souls along with our physical bodies, we can come even more completely into agreement with the Holy Spirit. You could say that our bodies and minds begin to experience an increased measure of the reality that our spirits already experience in the Lord's presence.

Praying in the Spirit gives the Holy Spirit the opportunity to teach us how to think and pray. Jesus explained to His disciples that after He ascended the Father would send the Spirit for this specific purpose:

> *However, when He, the Spirit of truth, has come, He will guide you into all truth; for He will not speak on His own authority, but whatever He hears He will speak; and He will tell you things to come. He will glorify Me, for He will take of what is Mine and declare it to you* (John 16:13-14).

This is a glorious promise, but we have to understand that the Holy Spirit is not speaking on a megaphone, nor is His the only voice vying for our attention. In order to connect our minds to the frequency on which His voice can be heard, we must first dial down the voice of our own thoughts and wait to hear Him. I call it "leaning into His voice." Praying in tongues is a powerful tool that can turn our focus away from the things that distract us while at the same time helping us to become aware of His presence.

This posture invites the Spirit of revelation to enlighten the *"eyes of our understanding"* (see Eph. 1:18), so that we don't try to use our own limited understanding to explain what we see around us.

The wonderful gift of tongues allows us to pray with the Lord even when we lack understanding, and by drawing us into the presence of the Lord and enabling our minds to perceive what the Spirit is saying, we enter into greater comprehension of what He is doing and why.

When we move into praying with our understanding as well as praying in the Spirit, we further increase the level of our agreement with God in prayer. Paul wrote, *"I will pray with the spirit, and I will also pray with the understanding"* (1 Cor. 14:15). This is how praying in the Spirit builds our faith.

As we pray in tongues, bypassing our human intellect, the Spirit activates our faith; faith does not originate in our minds. Our faith connects us with the spiritual flow that is coming from God. Jesus said that He only did what He saw His Father doing and He said what He heard His father saying (see John 5:19; 12:49). Everything He did and said was in complete agreement with His Father. In other words, everything He did and said was done with perfect faith. His faith released the reality of His Father's Kingdom into the circumstances around Him.

That is the kind of constant connection to the presence of God (which sustains an increasing understanding of who God is and the way He moves) that is the heart of any believer's faith. Thus, the end result of praying in the Spirit and allowing such prayers to inform our understanding is that we can actually start to think and act like Him.

Instead of "praying" by tossing prayer requests up to the ceiling and hoping one will "stick" and bring an answer, the prayer of faith always gets results. The prayer of faith comes from the heart of the Father. Because we have drawn close to His heart and we have heard Him talk about what He wants to do, we know what to pray and how to pray. From this "inside knowledge," it is relatively easy to stand in the position of a delegated authority as His co-laborer and to declare what He has just said into the circumstances around us.

I believe that God desires every believer to mature to the point that he or she can increasingly see what the Father is doing, hear what He is saying, and step out in faith to agree with Him. As we learn to do this, we will find that while getting answers to prayer is always wonderful and important, hearing His voice in the intimacy of prayer is the best thing of all.

Points to Ponder

1. See if you can explain in your own words how praying in the Spirit gives the Holy Spirit the opportunity to teach you how to think and pray.

    ....

    ....

    ....

2. If quenching the Spirit means stopping His flow (see 1 Thess. 5:19 and the Meditation on Chapter 15 of this book), how might you have quenched Him recently? Bring yourself humbly to Him and repent, asking Him to remind you to spend more time leaning into Him, paying attention to His voice.

    ....

    ....

    ....

3. What has God appointed *you* to build in His Kingdom? How has He strengthened and helped you? In the process, what have you learned about leaning on Him?

    ....

    ....

    ....

    ....

Meditation

Expecting the Spirit to activate your own spirit, spend some time in private, worshiping and praying in the language He has given you. If you have never prayed in tongues, ask Him to release this gift in you. Remember Jesus' words:

Everyone who asks receives, and he who seeks finds, and to him who knocks it will be opened. If a son asks for bread from any father among you, will he give him a stone? Or if he asks for a fish, will he give him a serpent instead of a fish? Or if he asks for an egg, will he offer him a scorpion?…How much more will your heavenly Father give the Holy Spirit to those who ask Him! (Luke 11:10-13)

Now, steadily and gradually, "lean into" the Father's voice. Quiet your own thoughts. Listen with your heart. He is whispering something to you and He wants you to hear it.

Chapter 18

BECOMING CHILDREN OF LIGHT
Danny SILK

Many Christians believe that the nature of humankind is hopelessly dark. They have lingered too long on the Old Testament line, *"The heart is deceitful above all things, and desperately wicked; who can know it?"* (Jer. 17:9). When they read Paul's declaration, *"For you were once darkness, but now you are light in the Lord. Walk as children of light…"* (Eph. 5:8), they get stuck in the first half of the revelation, failing to cultivate the truth that we are truly "children of light."

Yes, we once *were* darkness, but that nature has completely changed. How can we get past our fear of sin and allow our offenses to be disarmed? When will we step fully into the light and allow Heaven to govern through us on earth?

When people sin, it is offensive. When someone breaks the rules, call them *offenders* and we put them in prison. Our society is filled with sinners practicing sin, and naturally our society is caught in a relationship with the rules. Even lawlessness is a relationship with the rules; some people define their relationship with the rules by breaking them. Without a relationship with the God of love and light, the only option left is to live life within the confines of rules and regulations.

Offense does something to you. It justifies your withholding of love. I get to withhold my love from you when you have broken the rules, because people who fail are unworthy of love and they deserve to be punished. And when I withhold love, anxiety fills the void, and a spirit of fear directs my behavior toward the offender.

When we are afraid, we want control, and our response to the sin of other people is to adopt a set of controls that helps us feel like we are still in charge. That's why the typical practice in a family, a church, or a government is to require an offender to walk through a series of behaviors called punishments in order to prove that the family, the church, or the particular government is still in charge. In doing so, we help to confirm the belief of the offender that he or she is powerless to change and take responsibility for the behavior.

This whole business is just what Jesus died to get rid of. He has introduced a whole new world with a whole new way. Our challenge is to allow His Spirit to influence our thinking more than the ways of the world around us. In spite of all of our preaching about New Life, regrettably most of us fall back into rule-bound thinking far too often.

Two of Jesus' disciples, Peter and Judas, denied Him, Peter three times and Judas one time. Peter ended up walking out of his darkness into the light of love and forgiveness, while Judas did not. So what was the ultimate difference between them? The real difference between them is not in their sin, but in what they did afterward. This is vitally important. It is called repentance. But repentance only works when the person makes a heart-to-heart connection.

Repentance does not satisfy the broken rules. Repentance will not work in an environment in which we are protecting a relationship with the rules. In a rule-driven environment, repentance has a different meaning. It signifies your willingness to let me punish you. You are "repentant" when you allow me to inflict my punishments upon you. You did the crime, so you must do the time. The issue of the heart that led you to make the mistake in the first place is never dealt with, because the issue of relationship and love is never touched. When we practice this kind of repentance in the Church, we are allowing ourselves to be defined by the limits of earthly government. We have not allowed the light to shine into the darkness.

True repentance, however, is a gift that comes in a relationship. The gift of repentance makes true restoration possible. In fact, it is absolutely necessary in order to heal the relationship that has been hurt by the sinful behavior. True repentance can only come through a relationship with God in which we come into contact with the grace of God to change.

When God restores someone who has repented, He reestablishes a royal family member in his or her place of honor. The restored believer can say, "I am now a son of God again." Restoration for the believer is always a restoration of relationship, because restoration is defined by the cross. Restoration to relationship is what the cross did. After John declared that Jesus had become the propitiation for our sins, he concluded, *"If God so loved us"*—that is, if God was so willing to protect His relationship with us, instead of protecting our relationship with His rules— *"we also ought to love one another"* (1 John 4:11).

The standard of the government of Heaven is that we learn to cultivate and protect our relationship with God, with love, and with each other. And if we can't do it, we won't reflect Heaven to the society we live in. We will just have stricter rules that offend us quicker, and we will judge more often and become famous for being offended judges.

In the Church, we have tended to paint everybody with the same brush. We say we believe in repentance and restoration, but we have a limited, earthbound view of what that means. When, through the wisdom of God, leaders can lead a sinner back into the light of their Father's countenance, that believer's life is changed. The light keeps shining. They move from glory to glory. I'm not saying that we give everybody a "get out of jail free" card. But instead of punishing them and crushing them even further into the life of a sinner, we can call people to walk in their higher identity and responsibility as children of light.

Points to Ponder

1. "Repentance"—what does that word do inside of you? Does it tie your soul in knots? Dissolve you in tears? Leave you cold? Remind you of past experiences? (Good ones or bad ones.) Do you feel you understand what true repentance is? How about true restoration?

   ....

   ....

   ....

2. Do a word study of the word "repentance" in Scripture. Look especially for verses that expand your current understanding of the gift of repentance, changing from darkness to light, and true restoration. (Some possibilities include: Romans 2:4; 2 Corinthians 7:9; 2 Corinthians 7:10; 2 Timothy 2:25; Hebrews 6:1; 2 Peter 3:9.)

   ....

   ....

   ....

Meditation

Your life as a son or daughter of the King, life in the Spirit, is intended to contribute to the global unveiling of the glory of God on His family. All of creation is waiting for this unveiling:

For the creation was subjected to futility, not willingly, but because of Him who subjected it in hope; because the creation itself also will be delivered from the bondage of corruption into the glorious liberty of the children of God (Romans 8:20-21).

The revelation of the glory of God in us is directly tied to the restoration of all creation to its original purpose. That is the hope of Heaven. That is how high the stakes have been raised. So it is not a matter to be taken lightly when one of us undercuts the flow of resurrection life by effectively denying the work of the cross and holding onto our old identity. We need to make a point of helping each other to walk out of darkness and into His light.

Chapter 19

PURSUING YOUR DESTINY
KRIS VALLOTTON

FOR MANY OF US, the most disconcerting thing about the incongruity between the Bible and our own experience is not that most of the Church still has a much lower success rate than Jesus, who healed, delivered, and forgave everyone who came to Him for help, without exception. What bothers us—and should bother us—is the fact that Jesus made the following promise:

> *Most assuredly, I say to you, he who believes in Me, the **works that I do** he will do also; and **greater works** than these he will do, because I go to My Father* (John 14:12, emphasis added).

Studied in its context, there is no possibility that Jesus can be referring to anything but the miraculous works that He had performed throughout His ministry. Likewise, He said:

> *And these signs will follow those who believe: In My Name they will cast out demons; they will speak with new tongues; they will take up serpents; and if they drink anything deadly, it will by no means hurt them; they will lay hands on the sick, and they will recover* (Mark 16:17-18).

You will notice that in both of these statements, Jesus identifies those who will perform these works and signs as "believers." We usually use that term to describe people who go to church, read their Bibles, and pray, but the life of the believer is to be marked by much more; it is to be marked by doing the supernatural works of Jesus. Our destiny to pursue the particular assignments that God gives us, and it only makes sense that much of what He wants us to do would be miraculous.

After all, the life of the believer begins with a miracle. The Spirit of resurrection brings us to life at our conversion, and all of us experience the superior reality of the Kingdom as it begins to empower us to leave our old habits, receive healing from the past, and be filled with peace and joy. It is only natural for those who have been raised from the dead and filled with the Spirit of God Himself to demonstrate the reality of their Father's Kingdom. The whole Christian life is miraculous.

Jesus declared, *"As the Father has sent me, I also send you"* (John 20:21). We are the representatives of Christ in the same way that Christ represented the Father to us. Thus, it is our destiny as believers to close the gap between the reality of our Father's Kingdom and the visible world around us. Everything that Jesus had available to Him is available to us. God has set us up for success in every area.

There are four things we must do if we are going to grow up into our destiny to walk in the supernatural. First, we need to be convinced that it is our destiny. Otherwise, we will hear the statement that those who believe in Christ will do greater works—like the statement that those who love Him obey His commands—as an impossible standard designed to expose just how far we fall short of being like Christ. Second, we must avoid developing a negative focus by looking at where we are not, who we are not, and what is not going on in our lives. Third, we must guard our hearts against disappointment and unbelief as we contend for breakthrough and experience confusing results. Last, we must feed our hearts and minds on the promises of God and renew our willingness to step out in faith and obedience in our daily lives.

A wrong focus, a failure to maintain a posture of faith through feeding on promises, and disappointment are all dealt with in the same way:

repentance. In repentance, the harmful pattern is broken and grace is available to start fresh in pursuing your destiny.

Many in the Body of Christ are in the same state Saul was in; we have been anointed as kings and priests, we have been commanded to disciple nations, and we have been equipped with the wisdom, power, and authority of God Himself. Yet somehow we find ourselves following some silly oxen around the farm, going back to our old habits, and focusing on survival when we have been called to lead and influence people for the Kingdom.

Because it is our destiny to do the impossible, it should not surprise us when God calls us to do something outrageous, risky, and unheard-of. Imagine what Saul must have felt like being called to the powerful role of kingship in his nation, a role that had never even existed before. Imagine how Abraham must have felt when he was called to leave his father's house to wander around in the desert until God brought him to the land of his destiny. Imagine how Mary felt, being asked to bear a child out of wedlock in the midst of a culture where most people would accuse her of telling a blasphemous lie to cover her immorality. On this side of their decisions, of course, we see how crucial their obedience and faith in God turned out to be. But we do not always see the same truth when God presents us with the assignments He has for us.

Every God-assignment is connected to His will, expressed by Jesus in His prayer, *"Your Kingdom come. Your will be done on earth as it is in heaven"* (Matt. 6:10). Whether it is leading a country or having a baby, a God-assignment is designed to release the reality of His Kingdom on earth as it is in Heaven, displacing the effects of the kingdom of darkness and bringing restoration.

Our faithfulness in carrying out our assignments is how we partner with God to reverse the effects of sin and death in people's lives, to restore the knowledge of the one true God. We restore supernatural signs of God. We restore health to people's bodies, souls, and spirits. We restore relationships and families, as well as prosperity, morality, holiness, and more.

Points to Ponder

1. What do you tend to focus on in your life with God—what you are *not* instead of who you are, or what God is *not* doing rather than what He is doing? What kind of unbelief does this represent? Consider how repentance could help you regain your confidence that you are moving toward your destiny in God.

....

....

....

2. Have you received a call from God to do something that seems totally irrational from the world's perspective? Or do you dream of doing something that has never been done before? How are you pursuing this call or dream? What might be holding you back from stepping into it?

....

....

....

Meditation

Did you used to be more passionate about the manifestations of the Kingdom of God than you are now? If so, would you say that this change is related to a lighter "diet" of feeding on the promises of God, or perhaps to dwelling on your disappointment when you didn't see a breakthrough?

You can turn this around. Repent and enjoy the freedom to once again pursue your high calling in Christ Jesus.

Forgetting those things which are behind and reaching forward to those things which are ahead, I press toward the goal for the prize of the upward call of God in Christ Jesus (Philippians 3:13-14).

Chapter 20

When God Colors Outside the Lines
Bill Johnson

THE KINGDOM OF HEAVEN has been breaking into our world with regularity in salvations, healings, and deliverances. The manifestations of that invasion vary. They are quite fascinating, and too numerous to catalog. While some are difficult to understand at first glance, we are encouraged to see them, because we know God always works redemptively.

Over the past years, on many occasions laughter has filled a room, bringing healing to broken hearts. Gold dust sometimes covers people's faces, hands, or clothing during worship or ministry times. Oil sometimes appears on the hands of His people; it seems to happen especially among children. A wind has come into a room that has no open windows, doors, or vents. At some locations, believers have seen an actual cloud of His presence appearing over the heads of worshiping people. We've also had the fragrance of Heaven fill a room. In my own experience, the fragrance of Heaven filled our car while Beni and I were worshiping on a short trip. It lasted for about 30 minutes, and it was a smell that I could actually taste, similar to having sugar granules sprinkled on my tongue. I have seen the small gems that suddenly appear in people's hands as they worship God.

Since early in 1998 we have had feathers falling in our meetings. At first I thought birds were getting into our air conditioning ducts. But then they started falling in other rooms of the church not connected with the same ductwork. They now fall almost anywhere we go—airports, homes, restaurants, offices, and the like. I mention this phenomenon in particular because it seems to offend even many people who fully embrace the renewal that God has been sending. It can be too easy, once we have made some adjustments in our belief system about what God will do, to think that we have now stretched far enough. Nothing could be further from the truth. Like the generations before us, we skirt dangerously close to regulating God's work by producing a "new and revised list of acceptable manifestations." No longer is it just tears during a special song or a time of repentance following a moving sermon. Our new list includes falling, shaking, laughter. The problem is—it is still a list. And God will violate it. He must.

We need to learn to recognize His move by recognizing His presence. Our lists are only good for revealing our present understanding or experience. While I don't seek to promote strange manifestations or to go after novelty, I do refuse to be embarrassed over what God is doing. The list that keeps us from certain types of errors also keeps us from certain types of victories.

The manifestations of God's power, while offensive to the minds of many, are limitless in number, and they are indicators of God's presence and purpose. Why are they necessary? Because He wants to take us farther, and we can only get there by following signs. Our current understanding of Scripture can take us only so far.

Remember, signs are realities that point to a great reality. If He is giving us signs, who are we to say they are unimportant? Some people fear "sign worship." While their reasoning may be noble in intent, it is foolish to think that I can carry out my assignment from God and ignore God's personal notes along the way. In the natural, we use signs to help us find a city, a particular restaurant, or a place of business. It's simply practical. In the same way, signs and wonders are a natural part of the Kingdom of God. They're how God gets us from where we are to where we need to be. That's their purpose. Had the wise men not followed the star they would never have seen Jesus.

There's a difference between worshiping signs and following signs. The first is forbidden, and the latter is essential. When we follow His signs to the greater depths in God, His signs will follow us in greater measure. Something has happened in me that will not let me accept a gospel that is not backed with signs and wonders. I did not go looking for a revelation of miracles on the earth. It came looking for me, and captured me. I have discovered that there is no lasting satisfaction in life apart from expressions of faith, and the way God "colors outside the lines" keeps my faith in hot pursuit of Him.

Sometimes when I teach on pursuing a gospel of power a person will follow my message with an affirmation of our need for power, while reminding everyone of the priority of knowing the God of power. True words, indeed. But sadly, such a comment is often religious in nature, meant to fend off the actual power of God, lest He disrupt their tidy worldview. A person who has a passion for the power and glory of God intimidates those who do not.

I know that my hunger for His power is only surpassed by my desire for Him. Certainly it has been my pursuit of Him that has led me to this passion for an authentic gospel, backed with signs and wonders.

I've been a pastor for decades, but I didn't see miracles, signs, or wonders for most of that time. I believed in healing and deliverance, but I did not have any success with them. I had correct doctrine, but not correct practice. However, a number of years ago God began to take us on a journey, giving us fresh Kingdom eyes to see what normal Christian living ought to be. Having missed much of the main activity of the Kingdom for so long, we were eager to plunge in to whatever He wanted to do.

I have come to see that the normal Christian life means miracles, spiritual intervention, and revelation. Written into the spiritual DNA of every believer is an appetite for the impossible that cannot be ignored or wished away.

Points to Ponder

1. Can you point to signs and wonders in your firsthand experience? In what way have signs and wonders directed you toward God's Kingdom?

   ....

   ....

   ....

2. Have you, or people that you know, found yourself being offended by something that could be a sign or a wonder? Can you figure out what about it bothered you (or them)? Do you think that your approach to signs and wonders has become a hindrance to your progress, or a help?

   ....

   ....

   ....

Meditation

Signs and wonders go hand in hand with the Gospel message. Paul spoke of the many amazing things that God had accomplished through him, *"in word and deed, to make the Gentiles obedient—in mighty signs and wonders, by the power of the Spirit of God, so that…I have fully preached the gospel of Christ"* (Rom. 15:18-19). The writer of the book of Hebrews stated:

> *How shall we escape if we neglect so great a salvation, which at the first began to be spoken by the Lord, and was confirmed to us by those who heard Him, God also bearing witness both with signs and wonders, with various miracles, and gifts of the Holy Spirit, according to His own will?* (Hebrews 2:3-4)

From reading the book of Acts, you know what some of those signs and wonders were. Use your Spirit-inspired imagination to transplant some of those phenomenal occurrences to the milieu of your present-day world. Now take some of the signs and wonders from the chapter above and imagine them happening in the book of Acts. Allow your expectations to expand!

Chapter 21

One Hundred Percent Success
Kevin Dedmon

I USED TO HAVE 100 percent success in healing; everyone I prayed for was healed. The catch is: I didn't pray for anyone, so no one ever got healed. During the first three years of my Christian life, however, I had prayed for many people and several were healed. One day I was called on to pray for a woman who had cancer. I went full of faith and prayed for the woman, fully expecting her to improve. That night, however, I found out she had died shortly after I prayed for her. I was devastated. I was overcome with the idea that I had killed her because I really did not have a gift of healing and should have summoned the assistance of someone who did.

I spent the next 23 years avoiding praying for the sick. I believed in healing, and I believed that the Kingdom of God could break into this earthly realm. I just did not believe that I could administrate the grace of healing because I did not have the gift. As a pastor, if I knew of someone who was sick, I would call on one of the "gifted ones" in the church. I would often quip, "You don't want me to pray for you. I might kill you!"

I truly believed people were better served if I did not pray for them. Then one day the Lord got my attention with a question: "Kevin, do you really believe you have the power to cause someone to die?"

"No, Lord, of course not," I responded.

"Then you do not have the power to heal someone either," He countered.

I got the point. Our job is to bring God's Kingdom to earth, which means that we represent His name in our lives. We are called Christians because we have taken His name. We are the children of God (see 1 John 3:1), which means we are to be identified with His name. Therefore, we have the power associated with the Name we carry, in order to meet any need we encounter.

Not only do I have His name, but Christ also lives in me so that He can live through me. In Colossians 1:27, Paul says that it is *"Christ in you, the hope of glory."* Therefore, I have what it takes to reveal the glory of God through my life. Jesus said in Luke 17:21, *"The kingdom of God is within you."* God is simply looking for those who will release what is inside of them.

I cannot save anyone, but Christ in me can save everyone. I cannot deliver anyone, but Christ in me can deliver everyone. Similarly, I cannot heal anyone, but Christ in me can heal everyone. Giving the Kingdom away is simply giving away the Jesus inside of us. Of course, in one sense I have as much of Christ as I will ever get, but in another sense, there is still more of Him being formed in me (see Gal. 4:19). So then, the more Christ is formed in me, the more I will have to give away. The ministry of healing is simply releasing the presence of Christ that is residing within us.

My breakthrough in understanding this principle came in January 2001. We had a young man living with us at the time who had been disabled for three months due to having ruptured a disk in his lower back while at work. He had just gone through surgery, but it had not helped. He had been left bedridden, and he was in constant pain. I felt horrible, watching him suffer in so much pain, without being able to help him.

One night as we were preparing for a fellowship group in our home, he asked for a few of the guys from the group to help him out to the couch where he could lie down. He wanted to participate with us and take his mind off the pain. However, he writhed in pain throughout the meeting, and eventually he became the focus of the meeting. Finally, he pleaded with me to pray for God to heal him.

Reluctantly, I yielded to his desperate plea. I figured his condition could not get any worse, and besides, there was no one else in the room who had the gift. So I was the best option available. I instructed the guys who had brought him out to the couch to stand him up. I went to him and hesitantly placed my hand on his back. I was just about ready to launch into a "comforting" prayer to help him in his suffering. But before I could, he yelled out, "Do you feel that fire on my back where your hand is?" Yes, I did. To my amazement, my hand also felt like it was on fire, and I had not yet even prayed!

A few moments later, he bent over, and then he jumped high in the air, exclaiming, "This is amazing! All of the pain is gone! I am healed!" He continued, "This is amazing….This is amazing!" and then he started crying, as he continued to jump around our living room demonstrating his complete healing. At one point, he sat down on the couch, looked up at me with tears of joy, and then jumped off the couch into a flying karate kick.

I was shocked, first, because he was healed as I had placed my hand on his back, and second, because my hand was still on fire, even though it was no longer on his back. Knowing this was a "God thing," I asked if anyone else needed to be healed. Two others immediately responded, and as I placed my hand on them, they were instantaneously healed.

In the process I understood that healing is not necessarily about gifting, but it is the released manifest presence of God—Christ in me, the hope of glory—His glorious presence released through faith.

Points to Ponder

1. Have you hesitated to pray for healing, as Kevin used to do? Have you considered healing to be something for *other* Christians to pray for? What adjustment to your thinking and faith has been provided by reading this chapter?

    ....

    ....

    ....

2. Perhaps you have not been hesitant, but have been avidly praying for others for healing, and have grown in your confidence along the way. How have you learned to be an effective avenue for the healing power of Jesus?

    ....

    ....

    ....

3. If someone should say to you, "You have what it takes to pray for my healing," what would you understand that to mean?

    ....

    ....

    ....

Meditation

As with the rest of your Christian life, physical healing is more a matter of releasing the powerful, loving presence of Jesus Christ than it is about knowing the right combination of techniques.

In a prayerful conversation with Him, ask Him to communicate to you more of His presence along with more faith so that you can keep following Him wherever He leads you, even into situations of direst need.

Ask Him to help you live in the truth of your sonship. It is out of this place of intimacy that you will understand how it is His good pleasure to give you the Kingdom (see Luke 12:32).

Chapter 22

Divine Encounters

Bill Johnson

FOR MORE THAN TWO decades, a driving force within me has been the conviction that *I owe people an encounter with God.* I owe them more than just a message filled with truth. Whatever I do for people must contain the opportunity for a divine encounter. If I am full of the Spirit, my preaching, my service, and my various forms of ministry will be more likely to bring people into such an encounter.

In part that is what the apostle Paul meant when he stated, *"My speech and my preaching were not with persuasive words of human wisdom, but in demonstration of the Spirit and of power"* (1 Cor. 2:4). People don't need to be convinced of our insights, our gifts, or our ability to convey truth. At best, these things are secondary in importance. What people need is God.

Encountering His power is encountering Him. Paul was so convinced of this that he wanted people to put their faith in the power of God: *"Your faith should not be in the wisdom of men but in the power of God"* (1 Cor. 2:5).

God is a God of covenant. He is confident enough and sovereign enough to bind Himself to agreements with His children. I prefer not to think of them as contracts, because that term is much too sterile. I prefer to speak in terms of relational boundaries. As we become like Jesus through obedience, we find that obedience releases His presence, His power, and His glory.

While I don't understand it fully, I am sure that He has a definite interest in our opinions and input. He promised us, *"If you abide in Me, and My words abide in you, you will ask what you desire, and it shall be done for you"* (John 15:7). It is foolish to think that He might want to make us into robots before He offers us the promise, "Ask what you desire." I believe that He actually *trusts* those who become like His Son. In that light, what could be more normal than for us to long for and seek out opportunities to display the power of God in lives of the broken people around us?

God cannot be properly or even accurately represented without power. Miracles are absolutely necessary for people to see Him clearly. Testifying about these miracles is part of the debt that we owe the world. When we speak, He comes to confirm what was spoken.

He has chosen to reveal Himself through people who yield to Him. His appearances are often spectacular and dramatic, as seen throughout history. His manifestations through His people may at times be similarly amazing, yet are often practical and normal.

I often learn by accidentally stumbling onto a truth. It usually starts with seeing the fruit of something before I understand it. I don't need to understand in order to obey. If you live to obey—no matter what—walking together with Him, this will become your way of learning, too.

It is acceptable not to understand Kingdom principles, as their power and effect are released through obedience. But if I don't understand them, I have less opportunity to be intentional in the release of His presence, and I am unable to train others to do the same.

The release of the presence of God, which carries in the Kingdom of God, happens through five actions that I am aware of:

1. *Laying on of hands.* This is a biblical mandate (see Heb. 6:1-2). The Kingdom within us is released through the touch of faith,

which is an intentional act for healing, blessing, or impartation (see Mark 16:18; 1 Tim. 4:14).

2. *Proximity to the anointing.* This is the principle that worked through the apostle Peter when the sick were placed in a location where Peter's shadow would fall upon them as he walked by (see Acts 5:15). Whatever overshadows you will be released through your shadow. This is what happened when Jesus' garment enabled the woman with the issue of blood to be healed (see Mark 5:28-29). The same applies to articles of clothing taken from the apostle Paul (see Acts 19:11-12). The anointing of God was upon Peter, Jesus, and Paul to such a degree that even their shadows and clothing became saturated with His miracle-working power.

3. *Acts of faith.* Faith requires an action. *Acts* of faith release the Kingdom. Think about how often Jesus was brought into a situation of need because someone else had faith and took action by summoning the Lord.

4. *Prophetic acts.* Prophetic acts often do not seem to bear any connection to the desired outcome. Consider what happened when Elisha helped the men who had lost a borrowed axe head in the water (see 2 Kings 6). When Elisha told them to throw a stick into the water, the axe head floated to the surface. In the natural, wood does not have that effect on axe heads, and axe heads do not float. The only reason God's power was released was because Elisha was obedient to perform the prophetic act. Physical obedience brings spiritual release.

5. *Declaration.* Nothing happens in the Kingdom without a declaration. When we say what the Father is saying, all of Heaven is brought into the equation. When that declaration is a testimony, we capture the momentum of the history of God's dealings with mankind. Then a creative prophetic power is released into the atmosphere to establish the revelation of God on the earth.

Declaration must become an intentional strategy of the last days' army. It is imperative that we no longer do this unintentionally or sporadically.

Rather, burning with the conviction that we carry the revelation of God's nature and presence for all to see, we must penetrate the darkness on behalf of a world that is perishing.

The Father has given us everything as an inheritance (see John 16:15; 1 Cor. 3:21). We will need everything in order to accomplish our assignment.

Points to Ponder

1. What principle of the release of God's power is in action when someone walks into a prayer-filled room and receives instantaneous healing?

    ....

    ....

    ....

2. What evidence do you have that you carry the presence of God wherever you go? Is this an attractive idea to you? How can you cultivate the atmosphere of Heaven right where you live and work?

    ....

    ....

    ....

Meditation

Your first action of faith must be seeking God in prayer, paying attention to whatever He says to you, allowing His Spirit to transform you progressively into the image of His character, and being obedient to His direction. Whatever daily actions of faith follow upon that will be determined by how much of Him resides in your spirit. Your part is to remain active, not passive. He wants you to be relational, not slavish.

Look around you right now. Evaluate whether or not the Spirit of God has had any influence on your environment through you. Ask Him what to do internally, externally, or both.

Chapter 23

Connection With God
Beni Johnson

WHEN I am really in that place where I feel completely connected to God, I have an instant peace. Everything makes sense and becomes "centered" in an instant. It is as if my spirit, soul, and body are saying, "aahhh."

Because I know what it feels like to be connected with God, I have become much more aware of how it feels when I've lost that connection. I have learned that when I am not walking in that connecting place with God, I begin to feel insecure. Everything begins to feel out of sorts, and I have to re-connect with the heart of God and His presence to make everything fall back into its right place again.

Another way I can tell if I am not connecting with God is that I begin to let outside influences affect my emotions, my spirit, and my decisions. That is because I am not connected to what is truly real (see 2 Cor. 4:18).

I have learned that I can experience the reality of the presence of God no matter where I am or what I am doing. He is right there when I am in my car, taking a walk, or playing with my grandchildren. And because I have spent time with God, focusing on His presence, I have found that I now have access to an instant connection.

The place of connection with God is the place of rest. We are supposed to be walking in rest as much as possible, day in and day out. The meaning of the word "rest" in both the Hebrew (*shabath*) and Greek (*katapausis*) is to "cease, celebrate, desist from exertion, leave, put away, repose and abide."[1] You can see the word "sabbath" in the Hebrew term. In a true sabbath rest, you must cease from your labors, your own efforts, and your own activities, but that does not imply that you must stop your ministry or work entirely. A true rest means having a heart of rest in all circumstances.

Sometimes a performance mind-set can take over and push us to do things for God that He is not asking us to do. Then we become restless—which means "less rest." When that happens, it takes us right out of rest. Whenever we begin to get that overwhelming feeling of restlessness and striving, we need to stop ourselves and enter right back into the rest of the Lord. We have to learn to give burdens back to the Lord. When we walk in this rest, we are able to live our lives more fully and we are more effective in using our spiritual gifts.

It is possible to carry rest with us because God is not asking us to carry the world on our shoulders. He'll do that for us. My husband is, I think, one of the busiest people on the planet. It is a challenge for him to get the rest he needs. But the one thing I have noticed through our years together is that he carries an internal rest of the Lord. It is very strong in him. He knows where his source is, and he draws from it often. If he didn't have that inner strength, there is no way he could carry on with his life. He has no plan "B." God is his plan "A," his source for everything.

We come to Him first, and then He gives us rest. Jesus said:

Come to Me, all you who labor and are heavy laden, and I will give you rest. Take My yoke upon you and learn from Me, for I am gentle and lowly in heart, and you will find rest for your souls. For My yoke is easy and My burden is light (Matthew 11:28-30).

Rest is mentioned twice in these verses. The first time, Jesus is saying *"Come to Me and I will give you rest"* and the second time He promises *"You will find rest for your souls."* As we continue to come to Him and to take on His yoke, we will learn from Him and grow in His ways. We will linger in His presence, and we will find rest for our souls.

Finding His rest is the by-product of coming to Him, and coming to Him must be an intentional thing on our part. It will not just happen. By the same token, returning to His rest is an intentional thing.

I remember one of the first times I began to practice moving into the rest of God. I was driving in to town to do some shopping. On that hour-long drive, the vehicle that I was driving decided to give up and quit. My first response was to panic and get really mad. "How could this happen? Everything is now messed up for the day." You know how we carry on sometimes. I found a pay phone (no cell phones then) to call for help. As I began to dial the number, I thought to myself, *Why am I acting this way? Why am I so upset?* Then I realized that something so simple had taken me out of rest.

I thought, "You know, I think that if I settle down and come to rest inside, I will be able to see what God can do in this situation." So I made a simple choice and decided to let God have this little mess of a day. Of course, once I made that decision, everything lined up and worked together. I chose the rest of the Lord that day.

I think about that day often. In what seemed like a trivial thing, God let me see that I could draw from His rest anytime I needed to. It is my choice.

God is calling each of us to choose His rest and to cultivate it in all that we do. He wants the stories of our lives to reflect His presence, which means that they will also reflect His rest.

Endnote

1. "Rest," *New American Standard Exhaustive Concordance of the Bible, Hebrew-Aramaic and Greek Dictionary,* version 2.2, Robert L. Thomas, ed.

Points to Ponder

1. How many times lately have you lost your rest? Did you realize what was happening? What did you do about it?

   ....

   ....

   ....

2. Can you remember a time when you intentionally chose to return to a place of rest? How much of a habit has it become to do so?

   ....

   ....

   ....

3. Give an example from your own life of "before" and "after"—without rest (restless, striving, agitated) and with rest (peaceful, clear-headed, calm). What were you able to accomplish with rest that you could not accomplish without it?

   ....

   ....

   ....

Meditation

What if you step right into the rest of the Lord right now? You can make use of words and prayers from the Psalms:

Rest in the Lord, and wait patiently for Him;…
Cease from anger, and forsake wrath;
Do not fret—it only causes harm… .
Those who wait on the Lord,
They shall inherit the earth… .
The meek shall inherit the earth,
And shall delight themselves in the abundance of peace
(Psalm 37:7-9,11).

Give ear to my prayer, O God,
And do not hide Yourself from my supplication.
Attend to me, and hear me;
I am restless in my complaint, and moan noisily,
Because of the voice of the enemy (Psalm 55:1-3).

Return to your rest, O my soul, for the Lord has dealt bounti-
fully with you (Psalm 116:7).

Come now into His presence; He is only one step away.

Chapter 24

LIGHT IN UNLIKELY PLACES
BANNING LIEBSCHER

I LOVE TO READ before I go to sleep at night. But I have never once headed upstairs to my room, turned on the light switch, and then waited as a battle warred between the light and dark. It's not that complicated; if I turn on the light, the darkness leaves. Darkness doesn't have an option. It doesn't hold voting rights. It doesn't stare at me defiantly and say, "I really like your room. I am not leaving." The minute light comes into the room, the shadows have to flee.

The light carried by every believer is the revelation of our King and His Kingdom. Jesus said to His disciples, *"As long as I am in the world, I am the light of the world"* (John 9:5). Then, anticipating His departure, He said,

> *You are the light of the world. A city that is set on a hill cannot be hidden. Nor do they light a lamp and put it under a basket, but on a lampstand, and it gives light to all who are in the house. Let your light so shine before men, that they may see your good works and glorify your Father in heaven* (Matthew 5:14-16).

Light reveals things. If you and I are supposed to be the light of the world, that means that we are responsible to unveil the reality of the Kingdom through every aspect of our lives.

The Bible is clear that the Kingdom is inside every believer (see Luke 17:21). It doesn't say the Kingdom is only within Christian leaders or only within those who carry a special anointing. If you and I really embrace this, it can mean some pretty radical things.

One of my friends, Chad, was on his way home late one evening when he decided to swing by a local grocery store to pick up a snack of donuts. On his way to the donut aisle, he noticed a lady in the checkout line who was wearing hearing aids. So he did what is becoming normal among us: He stopped and asked the woman if he could pray for her hearing to be healed. She explained that she had significant hearing loss in both ears and graciously accepted Chad's offer.

Chad prayed a simple prayer and then asked the lady if she didn't mind taking out her hearing aids to test her hearing. The lady removed her hearing aids. Chad stepped to one side of her, where she could not see him, and quietly asked, "Can you hear me?"

She said, "Yes, I can hear you."

Chad moved back farther. "My name is Chad."

She responded, "Your name is Chad."

He stepped back even farther. "My favorite food is pizza."

She returned, "Your favorite food is pizza." By now, tears were streaming down her face as she realized she was hearing clearly without the assistance of her hearing aids. She had been healed.

The cashier, who had watched all this unfold before her, began to cry too as she realized what had just happened in her checkout line. Chad turned to the cashier and said, "God is here right now healing people. Is it all right if I get on the intercom system and tell people what God is doing?"

With tears still in her eyes, the cashier replied, "Of course."

Chad grabbed the microphone and boldly announced, "Attention, shoppers. God just healed this lady of deafness." Then he had the lady get on the microphone and share her testimony of being healed. Seizing the moment, Chad began to give words of knowledge over the intercom system. "If you have carpal tunnel syndrome or if you are experiencing hip problems, God is here right now and wants to heal you. Come to cash register ten if you want to be healed."

At this point people were peering around the aisles to see what was going on. A small group began to form at cash register ten. As the crowd came together, a lady scooted up on a motorized shopping cart. She looked at Chad and said, "You mentioned someone with a hip problem. Well, that's me. My hip is in severe pain, and I am scheduled to go in for hip surgery." Chad asked if he could pray and release the power of God to her. Then he asked if she would stand up and test out her hip. She responded, "No way. When I walk on my hip, it causes excruciating pain." Chad coaxed her to her feet. As she reluctantly got up and began to walk, she started screaming. She turned to Chad with a huge smile on her face and declared, "There is no pain!"

Then, from the back of the crowd, a man pushed his way forward with his wrists held out in front of him. He said, "I'm the one with carpal tunnel syndrome. I have had it for two years. I've been in so much pain that I am unable to play the piano, which is what I do for a living. I teach piano lessons and am a concert pianist." Chad reached over, laid his hands on the man's wrists, and prayed for him to be healed. The man began to shake his hands up and down as he belted out, "My hands are on fire!" Instantly, the Lord healed him. His pain left and full mobility was restored in his wrists.

Chad spoke to the crowd that had just witnessed these two people receiving a healing touch from the Lord and told them about Jesus the Healer, who was revealing His presence and power right there and then. After giving a brief talk about the King and His Kingdom, Chad asked if anyone would like to give their lives to Jesus. Throughout the crowd, hands were raised as people surrendered their lives to Jesus.

Points to Ponder

1. What does it mean to be the light of the world? (See Matthew 5:14-16.) Does being the light of the world have to do only with evangelism? Name some possible ways that the light of Christ shining through believers could dispel darkness in the world.

....

....

....

2. In what ways have you been the recipient of God's light through a fellow believer?

....

....

....

3. Can you think of a way that the light of Christ has shone out through you in the past 24 hours?

....

....

....

Meditation

In order to shine with the light of Christ for the world to see, you need to be "plugged in" to Him. His light will not shine out through you simply because you believe the right doctrine or you attend church services. In order to plug in to the Source of light, you need to be giving your attention to His Spirit and choosing to engage in the give and take of your relationship with Him.

In many ways, His light and His love are identical. The more of His love you absorb, the more light you carry. It spills out of you. Sometimes people will even comment about it. You become a light source just as He is.

Chapter 25

LIKE FATHER, LIKE SON AND DAUGHTER
BILL JOHNSON

OUR HEAVENLY FATHER IS the Creator of all, and the Giver of all good gifts. His children should not only bear His likeness, but they should also be creative like their Father. When unbelievers lead the way in inventions and artistic expressions, it is because the Church has embraced a false spirituality. It is not living in a true Kingdom mentality, which is the renewed mind. The renewed mind understands that the King's dominion must be realized in all levels of society for an effective witness to take place. Someone with a Kingdom mind-set looks to the overwhelming needs of the world and says, "God has a solution for this problem. I have legal access to His realm of mystery. Therefore I will seek Him for the answer!" With a Kingdom perspective, we become the answer to every problem in much the same way as Joseph and Daniel were to the kings of their day.

Throughout much of Church history, people have been stripped of their God-given gifts, talents, and desires under the guise of "devotion to Christ." This stripped-down version of Christianity removes the believer from ministry and relegates that privilege to a certain class of Christian called "ministers." The regular believer's role is reduced to financial and emotional support of those in public ministry. While I am not devaluing the honor of giving to promote ministry, I am interested in putting the emphasis where it should be—on the importance of each individual believer carrying his or her own creative expression of the Gospel into the world around them.

Every believer is free to dream with God, to tap into the most creative force in the universe. To dream with God, men and women must learn to be co-laborers with Him. The desire of a true believer is never to be independent from God. The goal is not to find ways to shape God's thinking, as though He were in need of our input. Instead, it is to represent Him well, learning to display His heart accurately and instinctively through our giftings and our opportunities. His heart's desire, of course, is to redeem all people, and the tools He uses to display His goodness are gloriously vast, reaching into the heartfelt needs of every individual on the planet. Only divine wisdom can meet that challenge and only an army of co-laborers can reach into so many places so effectively.

We know that the Father's dream of redeeming humanity cost Him the life of His Son. Dreaming can be expensive. However, partnering with Him in His dreams will release in us a new capacity to dream like Him.

I am considering creativity not only in terms of art or inventions. In the Bible, wisdom and creativity are related. In fact, creativity is a manifestation of wisdom in the context of excellence and integrity. Wisdom is personified in Proverbs 8, and is the companion of God at the creation of all things. Therefore wisdom and creativity must not be separated in the mind of the believer. They are essential tools needed to complete our assignment of being effective witnesses to the lost. Wisdom gives us favor among the unbelievers in this world.

Although most Christians put high value on wisdom, most do not put an equal value on the role of creativity. Yet it is creativity that illustrates the presence of wisdom.

The six days of creation saw the most wonderful display of wisdom and art imaginable. As God spoke, worlds were made. Light and beauty, sound and color, all flowed together seamlessly as wisdom set the boundaries for creation itself. Solomon, the man known for his supernatural wisdom, described in one of his proverbs the co-laboring effect that wisdom had on that day:

Before the hills, I [Wisdom] *was brought forth;*
While as yet He had not made the earth or the fields,
Or the primal dust of the world.
When He prepared the heavens, I was there,
When He drew a circle on the face of the deep,
When He established the clouds above,
When He strengthened the fountains of the deep,
When He assigned to the sea its limit,
So that the waters would not transgress His command,
When He marked out the foundations of the earth,
Then I was beside Him as a master craftsman;
And I was daily His delight,
Rejoicing always before Him,
Rejoicing in His inhabited world,
And my delight was with the sons of men (Proverbs 8:25-31).

Wisdom is given an artisan title of "master craftsman." Note the emotional component: "rejoicing always before Him," "rejoicing in His inhabited world," and "my delight was with the sons of men." Wisdom is not stoic, as is so often pictured. Wisdom is more than happy; it is celebratory by nature and finds extreme pleasure in the act of creation.

But the greatest delight of Wisdom is in us! In humanity, Wisdom has found a perfect companion. You and I were born to partner with Wisdom—to live in wisdom and to display wisdom through creative expression.

In Scripture, the first mention of a person filled with the Holy Spirit is Bezalel. And what was his role? He was called upon to head up a building project for Moses. His assignment was to build God a house, so that He might dwell among His people. God had revealed what He wanted that house to look like, but it was going to take a special gift of wisdom to get it done. Bezalel was given supernatural wisdom to complete the task with artistic excellence. Wisdom qualified him to take on the assignment, and wisdom enabled Him as an artisan or master craftsman to design and build what was in the heart of God. (See Exodus 31:3-5; 35:30-35.)

Because of Jesus' Spirit, you and I not only can combine God's wisdom with artistic design and excellent inventive work, we also have the power of His Spirit to bring solutions to impossible situations.

Points to Ponder

1. How does creativity demonstrate the presence of wisdom?

....

....

....

2. Draw some parallels between God's creativity at creation and your own expressions of creativity. Broaden the scope to include many life-giving aspects of your daily routines. From your own experience, can you also draw connections between creative expressions and wisdom?

....

....

....

3. What are some ways that creativity and wisdom help establish the Kingdom of God?

....

....

....

Meditation

The devil himself has no creative abilities whatsoever. All he can do is distort and deform what God has made. In the face of the devil's efforts, God re-creates and creates some more, often through the lives of his people, which includes you. When wisdom and creativity become the normal expression of God's people, the devil's resistance against them is weakened.

God makes Himself known through His works. When His works flow through His children, their identity is revealed, and there is an inescapable revelation of the nature of God in the land. He becomes irresistible to those who have eyes to see, and those who oppose Him become disheartened.

His Spirit within you wants to find expression through your mind, eyes, words, and hands. Ask Him how you can be true to yourself—and Him—today.

Chapter 26

Thanksgiving—Agreeing With Heaven
Bill Johnson

Imagine Christmas morning. You've spent the last few months shopping for unique gifts for each of your family members, gifts that show your intimate knowledge of their interests and desires. You've spared no expense to get gifts of the highest quality that will be both enjoyable and beneficial to each person. But when your family comes to the Christmas tree, one person completely ignores the presents. Another person opens your gift, but starts using it for something other than what it was made for. Still another just holds the gift, refusing to unwrap it. To make matters worse, none of them even acknowledges that their gifts are from you.

Sadly, this is how many Christians respond to God's gifts, particularly the gifts of the Spirit. So many people fail to receive what the Lord has offered them because they don't understand what the gifts are or how to use them. They say ridiculous things such as, "Well, tongues is the least of the gifts, so I won't pursue it." If my children said this about one of the presents I'd put under the tree for them, I'd say, "This is yours! I don't care how small you think it is. I bought it with you in mind, and I don't give cheap gifts. If you'll just open it, I'll show you what it is and how to use it." Such a rejection of gifts is arrogant.

Thankfulness carries an attitude of humility. Thanksgiving is the only proper way to receive what God has given us because it honors our relationship with Him by expressing trust in His goodness, even if we don't yet understand what we've received.

God gives us *"every good and perfect gift"* (see James 1:17) for two primary reasons: He gives us gifts to make us prosper so we can succeed in life, and He gives to demonstrate His love as an invitation to relationship. Thanksgiving recognizes that the gifts we have received from the Lord came with these purposes. Thanksgiving sets us on course to know God and discover the reasons for which He made us.

Thanksgiving agrees with Heaven by acknowledging the truth that our lives are a gift from God, and that He is sovereign over all. God is extravagantly generous, and the life He has given us on this planet is not a life of survival, but of abundance and blessing. However, unless we properly recognize what we have been given, we will not be able to experience that life. That is the reality of receiving a gift. If we don't understand what we've been given, we won't understand its purpose and be able to experience its benefits.

Knowing God is not hard. It's actually the most obvious thing in the world. All you have to do is glorify Him as God and be thankful. This response, because it agrees with the truth, gives you open access to the vast treasures of the knowledge of God. But without that response, your thoughts become futile and your heart darkened (see Rom. 1:18-21). Futile means "purposelessness." When we fail to respond with thanksgiving for everything in our lives, our thinking gets cut off from our purpose in God. When we lose sight of our purpose, we'll inevitably make choices that are outside of God's intentions for our lives. Darkened hearts cannot perceive spiritual reality. Darkened, thankless hearts are unmoved by the desires and affections of the Lord, and therefore cannot respond to His invitation to relationship, which is the source of life. The absence of thankfulness leaves the door wide open to sin.

Since thanksgiving keeps us sane and alive by connecting us to the source of our life and purpose, it makes sense that Paul instructs us to give thanks "in everything": *"Rejoice always, pray without ceasing, in everything give thanks; for this is the will of God in Christ Jesus for you"* (1 Thess. 5:16-18).

Besides keeping us sane and alive, a specific dimension or thanksgiving is particularly powerful in times of difficulty and adversity. Simply put, thanksgiving *sanctifies* whatever it touches, even evil things. Look at Paul's advice to Timothy in First Timothy 4:1-5, where he tells him not to worry about food sacrificed to idols, rather to eat it after the purifying effect of thanksgiving has rededicated it to the Lord. When Paul says that thanksgiving sanctifies unclean food, he is saying that it sets it apart for God and His purposes. Thanksgiving actually changes the very nature of the food into something holy.

This truth extends beyond unclean food. It extends into every situation in your life in which you find other powers at work besides the power of God. Not everything that happens in life is His will. He didn't cause the crisis that an individual or a nation may be facing. He actually cannot give things that are not good, because he does not have them. God can give only good gifts because He is good, and He has only good gifts to give. So giving thanks in everything does not mean that the adversity came from God. But when you give thanks in the midst of an adverse situation, a difficulty that was intended to undermine your faith and even destroy you enables you to take hold of that situation and set it apart to God and His purposes.

When you give thanks, the weapon the enemy meant to use to dislodge you from your divine purpose is put into your hands and becomes the very thing that brings you more fully into that purpose. Jesus declared that He sends us out with the same assignment the Father gave to Him—to destroy the works of the devil (see 1 John 3:8). Thanksgiving accomplishes the divine justice of the Kingdom, where the enemy is destroyed by the very thing he intended to use for our destruction. Just knowing that we can participate in destroying the enemy's purposes should alone move us to give thanks!

Points to Ponder

1. In what ways might you have behaved like the family members who ignore their God-given gifts or misuse them? Can you see how these responses are not only thoughtless, but are deeply harmful to your relationship with the Giver?

   ....

   ....

   ....

2. Think of a specific example of a time when you made a choice that was outside of God's intention for your life. Tracing backward from the bad choice, how do you think you had failed to respond with thanksgiving for everything in your life, thereby cutting off your thinking from your purpose in God? In other words, how did you fall away from trusting Him? How did you try to take things into your own hands?

   ....

   ....

   ....

3. Have you had occasion to practice thanksgiving in a time of distress? How did it help?

   ....

   ....

   ....

Meditation

When God tells you to give Him thanks, He is not insinuating that He gives a gift to you in order to get something from you. He does not manipulate people with His gifts.

He wants you to thank Him because thankfulness acknowledges the truth about your life. And when you agree with the truth, then the truth sets you free to see and to manifest the greatness that He has put into you as one whom He has made in His image. When you withhold thanks from God, you actually cut yourself off from your identity.

In thankful prayer, start naming off things you want to thank Him for, including current difficulties and problems. Acknowledge His lordship over your life and everything in it. Rejoice as the truth sets you free!

Chapter 27

Combat Darkness with Joyful Worship
Beni Johnson

Two of our greatest tools of intercession are worship and joy. I believe that these two weapons bring more confusion to the devil's camp than anything else. Both of these weapons of war come out of our intimate relationship with our Father God.

The Greek word for "worship" is *proskuneo*. It means "to kiss."[1] Thus, it means a lot more than just coming to church on Sunday and singing some songs. It means adoration, from the heart. When we adore God, it is as if we are kissing Him. This puts our whole focus on God, which ushers in His powerful presence.

In one of our worship services one Sunday morning, I kept getting distracted in my spirit. I kept turning around to look at people to see if I could figure out a spiritual reason for my agitation. Then I heard the Holy Spirit whisper, "You are being distracted from Me; just worship Me." It was a little nudge from the Spirit, but I got it. I realized that what I needed to do was simply to be with God and to worship Him. He would take care of the spiritual matters in the room. My worship was a weapon of warfare.

When we worship, we have access to the heavenly realm. When we worship, we push ourselves out of the inferior realms where we pick up all of the negative stuff, and we end up in the glory realm, surrounded by His presence.

When we worship, we can release the presence of God and His Kingdom into the room. Worship, in whatever form—adoration from our mouths, dance, music, or any other kind of worship—terrifies the demonic realm. I believe the devil and his demons cannot stand to hear or be close to those who are true worshipers. I have watched our son Brian play his guitar over a person in torment to bring peace. I know of a woman who goes to the convalescent hospital in our city to play her flute over Alzheimer's patients until they become peaceful.

By the same token, true *joy* brings victory. We are supposed to be a people who are full of Jesus' joy in every area of our lives and ministry. One of the missing elements I notice in many intercessors is that they are not joyful. Their praying needs to become more like the intercession of Heaven. I would love to go to Heaven for a visit to see just how joyful it is. There, intercession is not labor-intensive. Heaven is a place of knowing and a place of pure joy. Jesus said, *"For my yoke is easy and My burden is light"* (Matt. 11:30). In other words, working for Him is a joy-filled experience.

To live like that may seem like an impossibility, but it is the most refreshing and effective way to do spiritual warfare. One of the tricks of the enemy is to get us on his level. Most of us have fallen for it. Satan's world is full of labor and striving. If we step into that world, we will experience burnout. That's the plan of the enemy, to wear us out completely.

Jesus' way is different. He said to His Father, *"Now I come to You, and these things I speak in the world, that they may have My joy fulfilled in themselves"* (John 17:13). His joy will be fulfilled in us every time we expect His light to prevail over darkness. We can shoulder any yoke if we know He is doing it with us.

We are releasers of His light. Simply being joyful is a wonderful way to bring confusion to the darkness that is trying to rule over you and others. Darkness cannot overtake the light. It does not understand it (see John 1:5). Just knowing that ought to give you extra joy.

As most people know, one important principle of any kind of warfare is the element of surprise. That's one way you can use this kind of warfare. The enemy does not expect you to be joyful. After all, this is war. And the enemy does not know how to combat joy in a person. He can't lay hold of anything. A joyful person is buoyant, even merry, laughing when the circumstances would seem to dictate crying. With a combination of worship and joy—sustained, joy-filled worship—enemy forces will be driven out and replaced by joy-loving angels.

Years ago we were doing some meetings in Alaska. For the first few meetings, we had some praise, but we never got into the intimate place of worship. We felt as if we had a wall between us and God. We had brought our lead worship dancer with us on this trip. She is fun to take on trips because of the joyful worship she expresses when she dances. When we want something broken in the spirit realm, we have her get up and just worship. She doesn't do it with warfare in mind, just with worship in her heart, but her dance of worship becomes war. We don't even tell her what is going on. We just want her to worship. We did that in one of the meetings in Alaska. She got up and began dancing, and whatever that wall was, it disappeared. Heaven came into the room.

Attending that service was a gentleman who could see into the spiritual realm. He told us after she finished what he saw. Earlier, he had seen demons sitting around the room. But when our dancer got up to dance, the demons began to scream, and they got out of the room as fast as they could.

Even so, we were not having our dancer worship because of its effect on darkness, but because God is worthy. With Jehoshaphat, we could say, *"We have no power against this great multitude that is coming against us; nor do we know what to do, but our eyes are upon You"* (2 Chron. 20:12).

Endnote

1. *The New Testament Greek Lexicon*, Strong's #4352. Studylight.org, s.v. "Proskuneo," http://www.searchgodsword.org/lex/grk/view.cgi?number =4352.

Points to Ponder

1. What kind of a weapon is worship? Offensive or defensive? Why?

....

....

....

2. See if you can describe in your own words why the gift of true joy works as a weapon against the enemy. Have you ever wielded this weapon on purpose? What was the effect?

....

....

....

3. Do you know someone who carries a joyful spirit wherever he or she goes? Or do you know someone whose ability to enter into worship draws you into worship yourself? If you do not know someone like this already, look around to see if you can find one in your circle of believing friends and acquaintances. Or become that person yourself, for the sake of the Body of Christ.

....

....

....

Meditation

Honestly, before the Lord, pour out your heart. Confess the burdens that you have carried that you should have given to Him, and then give them to Him if you still need to. Tell Him about how you forget to worship sometimes, and how you especially forget that worship might lift you out of your own gloom and into His heavenly light. Allow your honest conversation with Him to turn into worship, thanksgiving, and joy. Keep talking to Him until it does—and then keep worshiping as long as possible.

Cultivate a spirit of worship. You can enter into worship anywhere, anytime. It will make a big difference in your level of victory and, of course, in your joy.

Chapter 28

Drawing on the Grace of God
Danny Silk

WITHOUT a COMPLETE, MATURE expression of the graces that equip the saints, the people of God cannot be adequately prepared to contain the new wine that God is pouring out and to release it to the world around them. In any church, large or small, the "wineskin" of its leadership must be kept supple by means of the diverse anointings that come from various gifts. Each of these anointings addresses an essential part of the identity and purpose of the Church through their specific areas of focus and motivation.

In particular, I'm interested in what we call the "fivefold" ministry graces, described in Ephesians as follows:

And He Himself gave some to be apostles, some prophets, some evangelists, and some pastors and teachers, for the equipping of the saints for the work of ministry, for the edifying of the body of Christ, till we all come to the unity of the faith and of the knowledge of the Son of God, to a perfect man, to the measure of the stature of the fullness of Christ (Ephesians 4:11-13).

I am convinced that one of the reasons senior church leaders experience the disheartening cycle of great outpourings that gradually dwindle back down to business as usual is a lack of understanding of the fivefold ministry, of their own ministry anointings and callings, and of how their anointings shape the direction of their churches.

The five graces that equip the saints are apostles, prophets, evangelists, pastors, and teachers. What do they look like in action? I think I can best introduce the attributes of the fivefold anointings by describing what might happen if they were all to arrive together at the scene of a multiple-car accident:

> **The pastor** is the first one out of the car. He scrambles to assess the situation and begins a triage approach in applying first aid to injured victims. He gathers blankets, jackets, water, and anything else he can find to try to comfort them. He surveys the situation to see if anything is threatening the safety either of those who are receiving care or those who have been drawn to the scene of the accident. He talks with each person to find out his or her name, marital status, and whether he or she has children. He gathers vital sign information and any available emergency contact information in order to help the emergency response team when they arrive. He brings a sense of calm to the situation, and each person there feels a sense of his genuine care. The pastor wonders if he should have been a doctor.

> **The teacher** is next on the scene. He studies the situation in order to figure out what caused the accident. He steps back, notices the patterns of the skid marks and the distance each car moved before and after the impact, and he estimates the speed of each vehicle at the point of impact. Drawing from his deep knowledge of the driver's manual and traffic laws, he develops a theory about who was at fault. His conclusion is that, overall, drivers need more training. He decides to start a school.

The evangelist arrives on the scene and asks everyone lying in safe, comfortable places (thanks to the pastor), "If you were to die as a result of your injuries, do you know where you would go, Heaven or hell?" He notices that there is a large gathering of bystanders who have pulled over to watch. He begins to address the larger crowd with the same question. People give their hearts to the Lord right there on the side of the road. He explains to all these new believers that the greatest gift you can ever give to someone else is the gift of salvation. He trains them to lead others to Christ and prays for the baptism of the Holy Spirit to come upon them. Afterward, he says, "This was great!" and decides to purchase a police scanner when he gets back to town.

The prophet knew this was going to happen because he had a dream about it the previous night. Because everyone in the dream had survived the accident, he rebukes the spirit of death and declares with great faith that all shall live and none shall die. He also proclaims that there are angels surrounding the scene of the accident and prays that the eyes of all the people's hearts will be opened to see in the Spirit. Then he walks around and starts to call out the destiny in various people. He releases a spirit of revelation within the group. Finally and quite naturally, he begins to ask around to find out who is in charge at the scene. When he discovers the one in charge, he discerns whether this is God's chosen leader or not. Or if he finds that no one is in charge, he will appoint a leader.

The apostle prays for the injured. He invites the supernatural healing touch of God into the scene. He begins to tell testimonies of other car accidents, times when he has witnessed the power of God. The faith level of the people begins to rise. He asks if anyone can feel heat in his or her hands, and then he puts those people to work praying for others to be healed. Having demonstrated to all who are near that the Kingdom of God is at hand, he goes home and opens a school for those who arrive at car accident scenes and sends them all over the world to do signs and wonders.

No one anointing is better, more important, or more correct than another. Each anointing determines how a person will see various circumstances, and what solutions that person can bring to bear which situations. All five are God's gifts to His Church to help bring Heaven's perspective to the earth.

We need all five of them, working together. In short, apostles *govern*, prophets *guide*, evangelists *gather*, pastors *guard*, and teachers *ground*.

Points to Ponder

1. To be an apostle, prophet, evangelist, pastor, or teacher is a *calling*, whereas to minister in one of these areas is a *gift*. Purpose and direction come from *anointing*. Read the following passages with these distinctions in mind: 1 Corinthians 1:1; 1 Peter 4:10; Isaiah 61:1.

   ....

   ....

   ....

2. Do you feel that you have a calling to one of the fivefold gifts? If you do, whom can you point to in your church or in another church who manifests the same calling? What can you learn from that person about how ministry and anointing can flow with this gift? If you do not feel you have a calling to one of the fivefold gifts (which is fine—not everybody is supposed to be in a governmental role as an apostle, prophet, evangelist, pastor, or teacher), can you specify how God has equipped you to support the life of the Body of Christ? You have a calling, gifts, and purpose, too.

   ....

   ....

   ....

Meditation

"For the gifts and the calling of God are irrevocable" (Rom. 11:29). The gifts of the Spirit are permanent, but the anointing that gives them impetus will always ebb and flow depending on your current relationship with the Holy Spirit.

Your activity level will also depend, quite simply, on what is happening around you. You are part of a body, and all the parts of a body are not in use every moment.

Paul wrote, *"We have the mind of Christ"* (1 Cor. 2:16), which is plural. Together, we compose His body. Ask Him to help you fit better within the local body of believers, to help you stir up your particular gifts, and above all to grow in your relationship with His Holy Spirit.

Chapter 29

Smeared With God
Bill Johnson

We know that Jesus' promise applies to every single person who calls on Him for salvation: *"I am with you always, even to the end of the age"* (Matt. 28:20). Yet why do some people walk with a greater sense of God's presence than others? Why do some people place higher value on the presence of God than others? What makes it possible for some people to enjoy fellowship with the Holy Spirit throughout their days, extremely conscious of how He feels about their words, attitudes, and activities? Concerned lest they grieve Him, it is their passion to give Him preeminence in everything, and that passion brings these believers into a truly supernatural life in which the Holy Spirit works through them on a continual basis.

The difference is in the anointing. The presence of God is realized in the anointing of God. The word anoint comes from a Latin word that means "to smear." God's anointing covers or "smears" us with His power-filled presence. Supernatural things happen when a person walks in the anointing of God!

For the most part, the anointing has been hoarded by the Church, for the Church. Many have misunderstood the reason for God covering us with Himself, thinking it is only for our enjoyment. But we must remember—in the Kingdom of God, we only get to keep what we give away. This wonderful presence of God is supposed to be taken to the world. If it isn't, our effectiveness decreases. Does He leave us? No. But perhaps this phrase will help to clarify this point: *He is **in** me for my sake, but He's **upon** me for yours!* Not only is all ministry to be Spirit-empowered, it is to have a "gathering" element to it. Jesus said, *"He who does not gather with me scatters"* (Luke 11:23). If our ministries do not gather, they will divide.

The anointing equips us to bring the world into an encounter with God. We owe them that encounter. For that reason, every caring believer should cry for a greater anointing. When we are smeared with God, it rubs off on all we come into contact with. The anointing is most commonly understood to help with the preaching of the Word or praying for the sick, but it's the person with the continual anointing who opens up many more opportunities for ministry.

I used to frequent a local health food store. It was the kind that had strange music and many books by various cultic spiritual guides. I did business there because of a commitment I made to bring the light of God to the darkest places in town. I wanted them to see a contrast between what they thought was light and what is actually Light. Before entering, I would pray specifically that the anointing of God would rest upon me and flow through me. I would walk up and down the aisles praying quietly in the Spirit, wanting God to fill the store. One day the owner came to me and said, "Something is different when you come into the store." A door opened that day that gave me many opportunities for future ministry. The anointing upon me equipped me for service.

Jesus was walking down a crowded road with people from all sides trying to get close to Him. A woman reached out and touched His garment. He stopped and asked, "Who touched Me?" The disciples were startled by such a question because to them, it had such an obvious answer—everyone! But Jesus went on to say that He felt "virtue" flow from Him. He was anointed by the Holy Spirit and the actual power of the Spirit of God left His being and flowed into the woman and healed her. The faith of that woman put a demand on that anointing in Jesus. *"The anointing breaks the yoke"* (Isa. 10:27).

A very popular verse for receiving an offering is, *"Freely you have received, freely give"* (Matt. 10:8). But the context of the verse is often forgotten. Jesus was referring to the ministry of the supernatural. The implication is that, since you have received the Holy Spirit, who is the greatest gift of all, you must give Him away.

When we minister in the anointing, we actually give away the presence of God—we impart Him to others. Jesus went on to teach His disciples what it meant to give it away. It included the obvious things, such as healing the sick, casting out demons, etc. But it also included one often forgotten aspect: *"When you go into a household…let your peace come upon it."* (Matt. 10:12-13).

He has made us stewards of the presence of God. It is not as though we can manipulate and use His presence for our own religious purposes. We are moved upon by the Holy Spirit, thereby becoming co-laborers with Christ. In that position, we invite Him to invade the circumstances that arise before us. By looking for changes to serve, we give the Holy Spirit the opportunity to do what only He can do—miracles.

Give God a chance to do what only He can do. He looks for those who are willing to be "smeared" with Him, allowing His presence to affect others for good. Jesus said, *"If I do not do the works of My Father, do not believe me"* (John 10:37). The works of the Father are miracles. In the context of his miracle-working ministry on earth, He said, *"He who believes in Me…greater works than these he will do"* (John 14:12). I look forward to the day when the Church will declare, "Don't believe us unless we are doing the works that Jesus did!"

I owe the world a Spirit-filled life, for I owe the world an encounter with God. Without the fullness of the Holy Spirit both in and upon me, I will not be a surrendered vessel for God to flow through.

Points to Ponder

1. Sometimes "the anointing" can seem like a code word, which can diminish its meaning. In your own words, can you describe it? Include personal examples of both giving and receiving the presence of God because of the anointing (on you and on someone else).

   ....

   ....

   ....

2. How has the anointing helped you use your spiritual gifts to greater effect? Be sure to consider ministry gifts such as service and helps.

   ....

   ....

   ....

3. How can you carry God's presence with you wherever you go in the next 24 hours?

   ....

   ....

   ....

Meditation

Let the words you just read motivate you to seek His presence anew. Breathe Him in. Invite Him to change you some more. Listen for His voice deep in your heart. Surrender your whole self to Him again.

Ask Him to "smear" you with His presence, to anoint you so that you can carry His presence out into your world today. His heart is yearning to touch the hearts of other men, women, and children through you. Allow Him to have further access to your heart, and through your heart, to theirs.

Chapter 30

Practicing the Gifts of the Spirit
Kris Vallotton

I N THE DaYS OF Samuel, Elijah, and Elisha, the "sons of the prophets" studied under the guidance of these prophets in what was probably a school of prophets. Although the prophets were based out of Naioth in
Ramah, they wandered throughout the wilderness practicing their prophecies
while being mentored by these renowned prophets. (See 1 Samuel 19:18-20.)

Unfortunately, some Christians misunderstand the definition of practicing prophecy or any of the gifts of the Spirit. The truth is that we are not practicing so that the Holy Spirit can improve His gifts, but rather, we are practicing to improve our own ability to flow with what the Holy Spirit is doing.

In the book of First Timothy, Paul exhorts Timothy to minister in his
spiritual gift beyond his comfort zone. Anyone who has ever performed
physical exercise knows that there is little profit to exercising until your
body feels a degree of pain. If you wake up the morning after exercising
and you are not sore, you realize that the exercise only maintained your
current condition.

The same principle applies to your spiritual growth. If you do only
what is comfortable for you, you will fail to grow. Whenever you are truly
growing, there will always be an element of discomfort. You can look at

it this way: "The dogs of doom stand at the doors of destiny." In other words, the things you are afraid of often hold the greatest rewards.

Paul reminds Timothy to *"stir up the gift of God which is in you.… For God has not given us a spirit of fear, but of power and of love and of a sound mind"* (2 Tim. 1:6-7). He is addressing that fearful tendency in us. Whenever we step out in faith, we must step over fear. Fear is the guard dog that is protecting the fortress of spiritual prosperity. When the dog starts barking, we know that the treasure he is guarding is near. Most people do not step over the growling dog. The result: they don't grow because they don't practice flowing in their gifts.

Here are some practical suggestions for practicing the gifts of the Spirit, particularly prophetic gifts:

1. *Prophesy your day.* When you wake in the morning, pray and ask the Lord for information about something that will happen during your day. Write it down as clearly as you understand it. At the end of the day, check and see if the event that you prophesied to yourself happened. Also see how well you understood the specific details of the event(s).

2. *Practice words of knowledge.* Go to a restaurant or public place of business and pray for the person who is providing a service for you. Ask the Lord for words of knowledge for the person. It is usually best if you do this when the person is not in your presence. Write down the words of knowledge on a piece of paper. Later you can "interview" the person concerning the words of knowledge you received.

For example, if you think the Lord showed you that the person has three children, you can simply ask the person if he or she has any children. If the answer is yes, you can inquire how many, etc. When you are first learning, I would suggest you not tell the person that you have words of knowledge from God. In the beginning, this practice is more about you growing in your gift than about ministering. As your ability to hear the voice of the Holy Spirit improves, you will begin to step out in boldness and faith.

3. *Team up with another person.* Enlist the help of a prayer partner. Pray for one another and ask the Lord for words of knowledge for each other. Take turns sharing what you believe God has shown you. Let the recipient judge the word you are giving to him or her. Obviously, this works best if both of you are trying to grow in your spiritual gifts. It is important in this exercise to be extremely truthful with one another so as to gain an honest assessment of how you are doing.

4. *Practice words of knowledge for healing.* You can practice words of knowledge for healing in a group setting by simply praying and asking the Lord to show you anyone who is experiencing illness or pain. This will often come as a sensation in your body that directly coincides with the part of someone else's body that the Lord wants to heal. If it is appropriate in the meeting, ask the group if anyone has the specific problem in their body. Then afterward, you should pray for that person and experience the joy of seeing the Lord heal the ailment!

5. *Prophesy as a group.* Another way to practice in a group setting is to choose one member of the group and have the others prophesy to that person. As the words are given, ask a member of the group to write them down. After an adequate number of prophetic words have been given, ask the person who received the prophetic words to judge the words and give feedback to the group about the accuracy of the words.

6. *Prophetic intercession.* Prophetic intercession happens as we pray. Often in prayer the Lord will give you insight into people's lives. Prophesy the answer to each of these issues that you see in the lives of these people and then ask the Lord to let your paths cross that day. You will be amazed at how many times the Lord will bring people to your mind to pray for—people you haven't seen in months, or even years. Most likely, you will soon hear from them.

Practicing the gifts of the Spirit should take place in an atmosphere of love and a culture of submission to true spiritual authority so that we can be building on a firm foundation as we practice our spiritual gifts.

Points to Ponder

1. What are your spiritual gifts? If you don't know, pursue the discovery. If you do know, how are you employing them? How have some of them been shelved?

   ....

   ....

   ....

2. Decide on one particular method you want to employ to practice your spiritual gifts. Follow through with your decision and see if it makes a difference in your confidence and effectiveness. How will you be able to tell that you are growing in your gifts?

   ....

   ....

   ....

3. What is your greatest fear when you consider walking in the fullness of your gifts? What are you going to do about it?

   ....

   ....

   ....

Meditation

If you have learned how to play a musical instrument, think about how you became proficient. Even if you are a gifted musician, surely you had to practice from the very first day. And you know that you could continue to improve for the rest of your life; there is no end to what you could learn. In fact, times of intense practice (alone or in a group) provided the best preparation for whatever music you needed to play.

Put yourself into a situation that will challenge you to use your spiritual gifts as you nourish yourself with biblical teaching. Practice using your gifts. See if you can stimulate a spiritual "growth spurt" in yourself.

Chapter 31

GREEN LIGHT DISTRICT
BILL JOHNSON

Many believers live with the concept that God will lead them when it is time for them to do something. So they wait, sometimes for an entire lifetime, without making any significant impact on the world around them. Their philosophy—I have a red light until God gives me a green one. And the green light never comes.

The apostle Paul lived in the "green light district" of the Gospel. He didn't need signs in the heavens to convince him to obey the Scriptures. When Jesus said, "Go!" that was enough. But He still needed the Holy Spirit to show him what was at the forefront of the Father's mind.

He had a burden for Asia, and tried to go there and preach. The Holy Spirit stopped him, which also means He did not lead him. He then tried to go to Bithynia, but again, the Holy Spirit said no. He then had a dream of a man pleading with him to come to Macedonia. So he went to Macedonia to preach the Gospel. This is a wonderful story of God's leading (see Acts 16:6-10).

But it is easy to miss the point. Paul was able to obey because he was already in motion, carrying the Gospel into all the world. An adage comes into play here: It's easier to steer the car when it is moving than when it is standing still. Paul's commitment to the lifestyle of *going* put him in the place to hear the specific directions God had for him. The Holy Spirit was trying to keep him from going to certain places in wrong seasons.

Revelation is not intended to make us smarter. Insight is a wonderful benefit of an encounter with God, but enhancing our intelligence is not God's primary concern. His focus in revelation is our personal transformation. Revelation leads to a God encounter, and that encounter forever changes us. The encounters can be stunning experiences, or simple moments of being immersed in His peace. In any case, they are markers along the journey of "Thy Kingdom come...."

Without the encounter, revelation makes us proud. This was the reason for Paul's warning to the church at Corinth: *"Knowledge puffs up..."* (1 Cor. 8:1). The actual effect on our intelligence is according to the measure of transformation we have experienced. Revelation comes to *enlarge the playing field of our faith.* Revelational truth remains unproven theory unless it gets actualized through faith-driven experience. God wants us to experience the fruit of revelation about healing, for example, by healing people. He does not want us to use the revelation to develop a theology of healing.

"Revelation" means "to lift the veil" or "to remove the cover."[1] Revelation gives us access to the realms of greater anointing available to us to make that truth a personal experience and lifestyle.

The greater the truth, the greater the anointing needed to demonstrate that truth to the world. Anointing must be pursued, not assumed (see 1 Cor. 14:1). The measure of anointing that we carry reveals the measure of revelation we actually live in.

People ask me to pray for them to receive greater revelation. While it is always an honor to bless someone with prayer, these people seldom understood how revelation comes, or to whom it comes. The following is a list of practical suggestions for growing in receiving revelation from God:

Become childlike. Simplicity and humility of heart help qualify a person to hear from God; the desire to be profound is a wasted desire.

What many discover after years of teaching is that the simplest word is often the most profound. Jesus said, *"I thank You, Father, Lord of heaven and earth, that You have hidden these things from the wise and prudent and have revealed them to babes"* (Matt. 11:25).

Obey what you know. Clarity comes to the one who is willing to do the will of God. The willingness to obey attracts revelation, because God is the ultimate steward, sowing His treasures into fertile ground—surrendered hearts.

Learn the biblical art of meditation. Biblical meditation is a diligent search. Whereas religious cults teach people to empty their minds as a means of meditation, the Bible teaches us to fill our minds with God's Word. Meditation requires a quiet heart and a directed mind. When you mull a word over in your heart, pursuing truth in the same way that an inquisitive child's heart pursues a matter, that is meditation. *"I will meditate within my heart, and my spirit makes diligent search"* (Ps. 77:6).

Live in faith. Living by faith in your present assignment makes you ready for more. The light of the glory of Christ comes to the person who expresses faith (see 2 Cor. 4:4).

Acquire an understanding heart. An understanding heart makes a good foundation for something new to be built. God wisely awards fresh insight to those who have the basic principles in place. When revelation comes, the understanding heart has a "slot to put it in." It is not lost as seed spilled out on the ground. *"Knowledge is easy to him who understands"* (Prov. 14:6).

Give God your nights. I try to end each day with my heart's affection stirred up and directed to the Holy Spirit. What an amazing way to go to sleep. The Song of Solomon reveals this poetically: *"I sleep, but my heart is awake"* (Song of Sol. 5:2). God loves to visit us in the night and give us instruction that we would have a harder time receiving during the day (see Job 33:15-16).

Give away what you have already received. Continually giving is a sure way of getting more. When you are in "over your head" in a ministry situation, God draws out of the deep places in your heart insights that were not yet part of your conscious thought processes (see Prov. 20:5).

Become a friend to God. God shares His secrets with His friends.

Endnote

1. From the Greek verb form, *apokalupto,* Strong's #601, in *The New Testament Greek Lexicon*, Studylight.org (http://www.searchgodsword. org/lex/grk/view.cgi?number=601).

Points to Ponder

1. What was the most recent insight or revelation that you received from God? What idea just "came alive" when you heard it, read it, thought it, or realized it? So far, what have you done with it? How are you putting faith with it? How is it becoming active and having an effect on the world around you?

....

....

....

2. Do you live in the "green light district"? How can you tell?

....

....

....

3. When God gives you insights, how can you avoid the pitfall of pride?

....

....

....

Meditation

One of the greatest joys in life is hearing from God. There is no downside. But there is a cost that comes with the impartation. Part of the cost is the effort required to pursue Him diligently, and another part of the cost is the surrender of personal agendas.

If reading about the cost of revelation dampens your excitement about receiving His insights, ask Him what He wants you to change and how you can move into the "green light district." How can you cause your heart to become better soil for His insights?

If you feel you are already giving God a green light, position yourself for more. Ask Him specifically, for instance, to minister to you in the night through visions and dreams. Ask Him for more faith to accompany the insights He will give you.

Chapter 32

TRUE HUMILITY

KRIS VALLOTTON

RUE HUMILITY IS NOT the absence of confidence but rather, strength restrained. We cannot be humble by accident; we must purpose in our hearts never to exalt ourselves higher than we ought. Humility is an issue of the heart.

Jesus Christ was the ultimate model of humility and servanthood. He restrained His strength by emptying Himself of His privileges as God and by taking on the limitations of humanity. But the Gospels record that Jesus wasn't always perceived as a model of humility. Jesus regularly offended the Pharisees and even His own followers by making statements that struck them as arrogant and blasphemous. Here is a typical response to His statements:

> *Then the Jews took up stones again to stone Him. Jesus answered them, "Many good works I have shown you from My Father. For which of those works do you stone Me?" The Jews answered Him, saying, "For a good work we do not stone You, but for blasphemy, and because You, being a Man, make Yourself God"* (John 10:31-33).

The point is that the perception of other people really has nothing to do with whether a person is truly humble. Humility is an issue of how you relate to God and how He perceives you. Humility is a by-product of understanding and believing the truth of who God is and who you are in Him. We can be a people of humility and still be confident in our identity. Unfortunately, even that kind of confidence looks like arrogance to the insecure.

It is true that humility is a choice, but the fact is that the best way to choose humility is to choose to believe what God says about you. When we step out on the words we have heard from our Father, we discover what is truly inside of us and, consequently, we are able to learn how to restrain our strength. Faith is the most humble attribute we can cultivate in our lives.

John the Baptist was a great example of humility. He was a great man, and Jesus Himself praised him and declared that he was the greatest of all men *"born of women"* (see Matt. 11:11). He knew who he was and faithfully and boldly fulfilled his divine assignment to prepare the way for the Lord. But when Christ was revealed and began His ministry, John willingly stepped aside. He said, *"He must increase, but I must decrease"* (John 3:30). Was John putting himself down in this statement? No, because he didn't need to. He was simply stating a fact—when Jesus increases, everything else necessarily gets smaller. True humility comes from simply seeing ourselves in the right context.

So far we have been looking at seeing our greatness in the context of who God is. We also need to see our greatness in the context of its purpose. God has given the Church a great call, and therefore it takes great people to accomplish it. If we fail to see our greatness, we will fall short of our call. Our pauper mentality and false humility have rendered much of the Church ineffective by diminishing our vision for the influence we're meant to have in the world.

We have all encountered people in the world around us who are arrogant and egotistical. Some of these people have achieved real greatness in some area of life through developing their talents with hard work and determination. The tragedy in these cases is not that these men and women are taking all the credit for what they've done; it's that their greatness hasn't been directed toward the divine purpose for which they were created. Can you imagine what our world would be like if every talent and ability given to humankind was directed toward the praise and glory of God? Then the knowledge of the glory of the Lord would truly cover the earth as the waters cover the sea (see Hab. 2:14)!

In the parable of the talents, (see Matt. 25:14-30), the successful servants were those who understood that their master had entrusted them with some of his wealth to be used for the purpose of increasing it. This is what God wants us to understand about the greatness He has put into us. There will not be a question of our becoming proud when we truly understand and embrace the responsibility that comes with it. Instead, we will become sober-minded, disciplined, and passionate about developing what we have received in order to fulfill our calling.

The price that Jesus paid on the cross determined the value of the people He purchased with His blood. We were created to share God's glory and to bring Him glory. After all, who is greater—a king who rules over a bunch of bozos, or a king who stands at the head of a great army of confident soldiers who take pride in serving their king? Is it not true that the greatness of the king's subjects actually glorifies the king himself?

Even though David's first army was far from mighty, his personal greatness raised up those men to be like him, to the extent that 37 of those men have their names and exploits recorded in the Bible (see 2 Sam. 23:8-39). When they started out, it was an army of losers:

> *Everyone who was in distress, everyone who was in debt, and everyone who was discontented gathered to him. So he became captain over them. And there were about four hundred men with him* (1 Samuel 22:2).

In the New Testament, this scenario was repeated with Jesus and His disciples. When these men first came to Jesus, they were simply workmen with limited spiritual training. Under Jesus, they turned the world upside-down (see Acts 17:6). He trained them to do everything He Himself did and promised them that their works would be greater than His.

Their greatness came straight from the top. Their humility came, not from demeaning themselves, but from exalting their leader.

Points to Ponder

1. Why is it humble to believe what God says about you?

....

....

....

2. The fact that Jesus Christ humbled Himself in becoming a man obviously did not mean that He never displayed great strength and boldness. So what does it mean to restrain your strength?

....

....

....

3. Do you have a sense of the greatness of the call that God has put on your life as His son or daughter, or do you usually feel that you can't or shouldn't be a great person? How has a pauper mentality diminished your vision for influencing the world?

....

....

....

Meditation

King David made this statement: *"My soul shall make its boast in the Lord; the humble shall hear of it and be glad"* (Ps. 34:2). We have become so accustomed to hearing this line that we do not think very hard about the incongruity of combining boasting with humility. Yet it points out how boasting—in the Lord—can in fact be an expression of true humility. What we are boasting *in* is all-important.

Take some time right now and boast in the Lord. Worship Him, using the words of the Psalms and your own words. Declare His greatness. With your heart focused on Him instead of on yourself, enjoy the freedom of humility.

Chapter 33

It's Easy to Hear From God

Kevin Dedmon

F OR MANY CHRISTIANS, THE idea of hearing firsthand from God is very foreign. These same Christians have no problem petitioning God, expecting Him to hear their prayers. What they have difficulty with is believing that they themselves can hear back from Him.

Unfortunately, this means that many Christians have reduced "hearing from God" to getting an insight from the Bible. In addition for some, the thought of having God directly speak to an individual is somewhat scary, because of all the "kooks" who have claimed to hear from God, but who have obviously heard from another source.

Hearing from God personally is entirely scriptural. For example, Moses had a conversation with God at the burning bush, a conversation in which God gave him specific instructions to deliver the Israelites out of bondage in Egypt (see Exod. 3). Gideon gained confidence to take on the Midianites when the Angel of the Lord called out his true identity and gave him the confirmation through a "fleece" to accomplish his destiny (see Judg. 6:11-40). Paul heard Jesus' voice on the road to Damascus, and Peter had Jesus instruct him regarding the clean and unclean animals (see Acts 10).

Jesus promised that:

When He, the Spirit of truth, has come, He will guide you into all truth; for He will not speak on His own authority, but whatever He hears He will speak; and He will tell you things to come (John 16:13).

The Holy Spirit has been given to us to communicate the plans and desires of the Father. The Holy Spirit does this through visions, dreams, prophetic words, words of wisdom, and words of knowledge (see 1 Cor. 12).

It is easy to hear from God. Sometimes we hear from Him and we don't even realize it. That's what happened to the boy Samuel in the temple. God called out his name, and three times he went to Eli, the high priest, thinking it was he who had called.

I believe God is speaking to all of us more than we are discerning. I often travel to various churches, equipping and activating the people to live naturally supernaturally. Once I was at a particular church over a weekend. During the Sunday morning service, I called the leadership team up front to give words of knowledge for healing. We went through many words of knowledge, with several people getting healed as the words were spoken.

Finally, we came to one of the key leaders of the church, and I asked him to give a word of knowledge. "I don't have one," he responded.

"Sure you do," I encouraged.

"No, I really don't have one."

"Then make one up," I implored.

The congregation gasped, and the leader looked at me in disbelief, and said, "You're joking, right?"

"No, I'm serious; make one up," I pressed. The point I was trying to make was that hearing from God is a lot simpler than many of us imagine.

With a look of obvious consternation on his face, the leader grabbed the first word that came to his mind and blurted out, "OK, someone here has lower stomach pain, and you feel very nauseated." Immediately, five people raised their hands, and all of them were completely healed on the spot. The church erupted in praise as all five of them confirmed their healings in public testimony.

The notion that *"our thoughts are not His thoughts"* is an Old Testament statement about a rebellious Israel whom the prophet was beseeching to repent (see Isa. 55:8). To the obedient Christian, that statement should be changed to "Our thoughts *are* His thoughts." The Bible is clear: It is the unbeliever who has the depraved mind (see Rom. 1:28), and that mind is hostile toward God (see Rom. 8:7). The believer, the Christian, on the other hand, is commanded to be transformed by the renewing of his or her mind (see Rom. 12:2).

Moreover, the apostle Paul tells us in First Corinthians 2:16 that we in fact *"have the mind of Christ."*

Twice a year, we have "Pastors'/Leaders' Advances," a three-day event at which we have our second-year School of Supernatural Ministry students, who have been trained to hear the voice of the Lord, prophesy over these leaders. Two students per team, along with a junior high school student from our Christian school, will spend approximately ten minutes per person over a two-hour session.

On one occasion, two of our students were paired up with a 12-year-old boy. As leaders were placed in front of them, the two older students would look at each other, asking whether or not they had a "word." Each time, they would both respond that they did not have something right away, and then they would defer to the junior high student, who always brought forth lengthy, encouraging "words."

After the two-hour session was over, the two Supernatural Ministry students expressed astonishment at the competency level of the 12-year-old. When they asked him how long he had been prophesying, thinking he was surely quite experienced, he responded that this was his first time. Shocked, the Supernatural Ministry students began to inquire how he got so many words—words that turned out to be very detailed and encouraging to the leaders they had been prophesying to.

His response was simple: "My teacher told me that I was going to prophesy today, so I figured since I was doing God's work, whatever thought came into my head was from God. So when you asked if I had anything, I just said whatever first came to my mind." The School of Supernatural Ministry students received an instant, life-changing revelation regarding the simplicity of hearing God's voice.

Confidence in accessing and being activated in "words of knowledge" comes from (1) learning to tap into this "new" mind, the mind of Christ; (2) then, like Samuel, learning to discern that what you are hearing is actually from God; and (3) taking a risk to see if what you heard helps someone.

Points to Ponder

1. How many times lately have you received words from God that you have delivered to other people? How many times do you think you have heard Him for yourself? How many times would you *like* to hear from Him? Do you think you can hear Him more often than you are accustomed to?

....

....

2. Have you ever received a word from a "kook"? Have you become somewhat "gun-shy" as a result? What do you think God wants you to do about that?

....

....

3. Have you ever shared what you thought was a word from God and met with strong resistance or rebuke from the person to whom you delivered the word? In retrospect, do you think you made a mistake (which is normal), or do you think the word was in fact a good and accurate one? Was it encouraging? Had you listened to God to the best of your ability? What do you think God wants you to do with this remembered experience?

....

....

Meditation

Especially if you are surrounded by people who can hear from God, you may not listen for His voice as much as you could. You may think, "Well, someone with more experience and courage will get the word anyway. I don't need to try. I would probably mess it up if I did."

After reading this brief chapter, can you see yourself hearing from God more than before? Do you believe that you have the mind of Christ? Stop reading this book and start listening to Him now.

Chapter 34

God Hides Things for You, not From You
Bill Johnson

JESUS IS THE WORD of God. It's hard for Him to not have something to say. Occasionally, we go through times when we feel God is not speaking to us. Most of the time He has simply changed His language, and He expects us to adjust to Him.

The audible voice of the Father came from Heaven while Jesus was preaching:

> *Father, glorify Your name. Then a voice came from heaven, saying, "I have glorified it, and will glorify it again." Therefore the people who stood by and heard it said that it had thundered. Others said, "An angel has spoken to Him"* (John 12:28-29).

People acknowledged hearing something, but none of them knew what it was. Not only did they fail to realize it was the actual voice of God, it never occurred to them that this unusual event had any meaning for their lives. Jesus responded to their unbelief by saying, *"This voice did not come because of Me, but for your sake"* (see John 12:27-30). God spoke to provide a way out of the lifestyle of unbelief for every bystander, but hardness of heart made what they heard unintelligible. Some thought it was thunder—an impersonal act of nature. Others thought it might have been an angel—spiritual, but just not for them.

Unbelief can masquerade as wisdom, and it must be exposed for being the great sin that it is. Unbelief has the outward appearance of a conservative approach to life, but it works to subject God Himself to the scrutiny and control of people. It feeds off the opinion of others, all the while priding itself for not falling into the extremes that others have stumbled into.

Why do so many Christians need me to prove that God has actually done what they've seen Him do? When the miracles happen before their eyes, they still want doctors' reports and X-rays before they will give God any praise. Here is an empty wheelchair with its former occupant pushing it, or a formerly depressed person rejoicing, or a formerly deaf person giving praise to God for every sound he can hear, while the bystander demands proof that these were really miracles. I realize that charlatans exist. But the massive effort to protect ourselves from being fooled is more a sign of unbelief than it is of our wisdom.

The heart of abiding faith "leans into God," anticipating His voice, looking for His next move. Like Jesus, we can say, *"My food is to do the will of Him who sent Me"* (John 4:34). I am strengthened and nourished when I hear God speak and obey. Hearing from God is essential to the Christian life, for *"man shall not live by bread alone, but by every word that proceeds from the mouth of God"* (Matt. 4:4). His voice is our life.

In life, we can eat at the table of public opinion, where the food is sweet but it sours in the stomach. We can choose the table of personal achievement, a power meal for sure, a crash as rapid as the ascent. Only one table has rich food that settles well and brings supernatural strength; it is the table of God's will. The beauty of His will is lost for the person who does not know the language of the Spirit.

It is vital to learn how God speaks. His first language is not English. In fact, it's not Hebrew, either. While He uses the languages of men to communicate, He is more inclined to speak through a myriad of other methods. What follows is far from a complete list; it represents the limited discoveries of my own adventure with God:

The language of the Scriptures. The Scriptures are the basis for all "hearing" from God. While God will not violate His Word, He often violates our understanding of His Word. Remember, God is bigger than His book. The Bible does not contain God; it reveals Him.

The language of the audible voice. The audible voice may come to our natural ear while we're awake or asleep. It can also come to our spiritual ears. (I make this distinction because after it has happened, you can't always remember if it was out loud or internal. But it's far more than an "impression." It is as clear as hearing someone speak.)

The language of the still, small voice. This is the quiet voice or impression of the heart. This is probably the most common way that people hear from God. We can learn to distinguish it from our own thoughts and ideas. Someone once told me, "You know you have heard from God whenever you have an idea that's better than one you could think up yourself."

The language of visions. Visions come both to the natural eye and to the eyes of the heart. The second are the pictures in the mind, which are the visual equivalent of the still, small voice—they are as easy to miss as they are to get. "Leaning into God" is what makes them come into focus.

The language of dreams. Obviously, dreams happen mostly at night. But there is a form of dreaming that is similar to a daydream, when a person is awake. These are more likely to be ignored, because they seem like "just my imagination." In their more intense form they are more like a trance.

The language of dark sayings (see Proverbs 1:6). God sometimes speaks to us by hiding truths in phrases, parables, riddles, unusual coincidences, and circumstances. The meaning is there for us to find. When we lean into God, it becomes easier to discern when those circumstances are from God or are merely unusual events in life. This unique language from God is an invitation to enter His great adventure.

Having the heart and the ability to hear and understand the languages of God provides us with an unlimited potential for bringing the resources of Heaven to a needy earth.

Points to Ponder

1. Explain why this is a true statement: "The hungry heart hears best."

....

....

....

2. How do you most commonly hear God's voice? Which of His "languages" have you learned to listen for? Can you think of another language of God besides the ones presented in this chapter?

....

....

....

3. Have you fallen into the trap of unbelief masquerading as wisdom? What have you done about it?

....

....

....

Meditation

Even as you read these words, God is speaking to you. Without getting spooky about it, what do you think He is saying? Hold that thought and listen some more. Now what do you think He is saying about what you just thought you heard Him say? Really listen, expecting Him to surprise you with something delightful.

Hold onto what He has just told you. Ask Him to expand upon it, if necessary. Ask Him to mold your faith and expectation level as a potter molds a vessel. He wants to increase your capacity to hear His voice, day or night, full volume or quiet, in crowds or when you are alone.

Chapter 35

If It Matters to You, It Matters to Him
Bill Johnson

P ERHAPS YOU'VE HEARD IT said, "God is number one, the family is number two, and the Church is number three." That unofficial list is important as it helps to prioritize a Christian's life. I know of many tragedies in pastors' families because they ignored these priorities of Kingdom living. Yet, as good as this list is, I don't believe it is technically accurate. When God is number one, there is no number two.

Out of my love for God I give myself to my wife and kids. It's not separate from the Lord but unto Him. It's not that I cannot love my wife without loving God—many unbelievers do that well. But in knowing and loving God I am released to a measure of supernatural love that is unattainable apart from God. Anyone who is completely abandoned to God should love others more than they thought possible.

It is because of my passion for Jesus that I love the Church the way I do. My love for God *is* my love for life. They cannot be separated. Loving my family, church, ministry, etc., is an expression of my love for God, who is number one, the only One.

Religion destroys this connection because it implies that only overtly spiritual activities are acceptable as service to God. Religion takes us back to the concept of spiritual and secular parts of the Christian life. The person living this dual life needs a list of priorities to survive, but their concept of God doesn't allow them to actually have a passion for something that is not viewed as a Christian discipline.

We must have a shift in our thinking whereby we recognize that passion for God *gives birth* to a passion for other things. We should not experience them as something in competition with, or separate from, our devotion to God. John wrote that our love for God will be measured by our love for people (see 1 John 4:20). This is such an absolute principle that God says if we don't love others, we don't actually love Him. In the wake of our passion for God, passion for people and things is created. Often, in giving ourselves to those things, we prove and manifest our love for God.

In my case, my love of the outdoors is part of my devotion to Christ. While some worship nature, I worship the One it points to—the Creator. My love for my family, for hunting and fishing, the mountains and the ocean, fountain pens, and French roast coffee are all part of the enjoyment of life for me; and that joy is born completely through my relationship with Him.

Throughout Scripture, David is known as the "man after God's heart." His passion for God seems unparalleled in Scripture. At the same time, he also illustrates a love for life that is without equal. In Psalm 137, he calls Jerusalem "my chief joy." How can he make a city the primary object of his affections? Isn't God supposed to be his chief joy? This apparent paradox simply illustrates the idea that we must have a practical expression of spiritual truths. David's love for God needed expression, and Jerusalem was a perfect target.

While it is possible to value other things above God, it is not possible to value God without valuing other things. The religious mind-set dismisses everything not considered sacred, recommending a monastic lifestyle as a high attainment. While I admire many of the monastic believers in the past, it is not the model that Jesus gave us. In His view, the way we steward the rest of life becomes the litmus test for our authentic love for God.

Like most people, I have a list of things I pray for. They represent the basic desires and needs of my life and those I love. If they're not written down on paper, they're at least written in my heart. On the list are things that have obvious eternal significance—prayer for our cities, for the salvation of certain people, for healing breakthroughs in tough cases, for provision—both personal and for the church. Following the urgent is the "it would be nice" section of the list. It is long and the items carry varying degrees of importance.

I have noticed that God sometimes bypasses my higher-priority section and goes directly to the "I haven't even bothered to ask" part that dwells somewhere deep in my heart. On one such occasion a friend came up to me and said, "Hey, would you like a hunting dog?" I've always wanted to have a well-trained hunting dog, but never had the time or money for such a luxury. Nor was it on my list. He went on to say, "A dog trainer owes me a big favor and said he'd get me any kind of dog I want. I don't need another dog. So tell me what kind of dog you'd like and I'll get it for you." Just like that, I was to be the owner of a dog that wasn't on my prayer list. It wasn't even on the "it would be nice" part of my list. It wasn't important enough. It was, however, a secret desire in my heart. God bypassed all the stuff that had such eternal significance and went to something temporal and seemingly insignificant.

It offended me at first. Not that I wasn't thankful; I was. But it made no sense. I would have preferred Him to let me use that "trump card" for something that was more important to me.

It took awhile, but eventually I got it. My requests were important, but my view of Him was more important. It was then and there I started to see that *if it matters to me, it matters to Him.* What He had done told me more about my heavenly Father than I could have learned had He answered all the other requests I had on my list.

Points to Ponder

1. How have you limited God to your human way of thinking about priorities? Are you beginning to see things in a new light?

....

....

....

2. Does recognizing some misplaced priorities make you want to justify your assumptions and choices? How will you proceed? How will you relax into His loving care?

....

....

....

3. Do you know someone who exemplifies a rich and abundant life with God? Is that person interested in things, even avid? Is that person full of the joy of living? Let the example of such a person lead you into greater freedom yourself.

....

....

....

Meditation

Too often, people limit God to certain priorities because, deep down inside, they believe that His power is limited. It is hard to see, because they seem to be so concerned for the welfare of others. They say, "Oh, don't worry about my chronic illness. Ask God to heal my child instead"—as if He might run out of power or mercy after He heals the child.

He has enough power to heal both. We don't get just one or two wishes. He won't run out of grace. It's not an either/or situation. Besides, His attention span is excellent; so good, in fact, that He can give His undivided attention to every human being on the planet at the same time.

He cares about everything that you care about. Allow His abundance to flow into your spirit and soul.

Chapter 36

The Name of Jesus

Kevin Dedmon

THERE IS MORE TO a name than just a name. A primary key to releasing the healing power of God is found in the story of Peter healing the crippled beggar (see Acts 3). After healing the man, Peter addressed the crowd that was looking on, explaining the source of the power to provide the cure. He declared,

> *His name* [Jesus], *through faith in His name, has made this man strong, whom you see and know. Yes, the faith which comes through Him has given him this perfect soundness in the presence of you all* (Acts 3:16).

The key to bringing healing into people's lives was and still is the name of Jesus.

Regrettably, some people have been misled into the notion that as long as they put the phrase "in Jesus' name" as a tag to their request, whatever they have asked will be done. Some wield this phrase as though it is a lucky rabbit's foot: "If I just say 'in Jesus' name,' then it will happen." But it is important to understand that a name is more than a name in the Scriptures.

In the Bible, especially in the Old Testament, a name signified a person's nature, character, personality, and attributes, and it led to predictable behaviors. Whatever name used to identify God depicted a specific aspect of His divine nature, character, personality, and attributes. For example, Yahweh or Jehovah *Rapha* means *"the Lord who heals"* (see Exodus 15:26). This principle applies not only to God, but to others as well.

The name Jacob, for instance, means "deceiver." Throughout the life of Jacob in the Bible, we find him expressing his name through his behavior. Jacob deceived his brother Esau (see Gen. 27), cheating Esau out of his familial blessing, an action that necessitated his flight to his uncle Laban's household. While taking refuge there, he used deceptive tactics to steal Laban's sheep, which forced him again to flee (see Gen. 30-31).

Even Jacob's sons, Simeon and Levi, followed in his deceptive conduct when Dinah, their sister, was abused by the Shechemites. Simeon and Levi offered impunity to them if they agreed to circumcision. Once they submitted to the procedure, however, they were killed, even though a promise had been given (see Gen. 34).

Back in Genesis 32, Jacob had a wrestling match with God, which ended in Jacob being blessed with a name change. God said, *"Your name shall no longer be called Jacob, but Israel* [literally, "Contender with God," one who struggles with God and wins and is therefore blessed] *for you have struggled with God and with men, and have prevailed"* (Gen. 32:28). God confirmed Jacob's new identity later, saying, *"And God said to him, 'Your name is Jacob; your name shall not be called Jacob anymore, but Israel shall be your name.' So He called his name Israel"* (Gen. 35:10). The implication was that Jacob became blessed because of his overcoming.

In reading the rest of the history of Israel throughout the Old Testament, we find the nation of Israel struggling with God, and even in their rebellion they ultimately won with God and were blessed. Even today, God is working toward blessing the Jews through endless hardship and persecution. Israel is their name. Therefore, they cannot help but to be blessed, as it is their identity.

Along the same lines, among the many names used to describe the enemy, the name devil means "divider." The Greek word is *diaballo*, which means to thrust through the middle of something (*dia* = "through" and *ballo* = "thrust"), in other words, to split or divide something.[1] Division is what the devil does; it is who he is; you see the effects of his name everywhere. To accomplish his will, the devil stimulates and promotes slander, miscommunication, innuendo, insinuation, offenses, and other divisive tactics to separate what God has joined together.

Similarly, whenever we find a revelation of God's name in Scripture, it is an expression of His nature, character, personality, and attributes leading to predictable behavior. His name is who He is. His name is what He does and how He acts; His name is His very nature. So then, if His name is Healer, it means that healing is part of His nature, expressed through His behavior. That is why we can never say that God wants someone to become or remain physically sick or crippled. God is the Healer, not the Destroyer. Healing expresses who He is, and therefore Healing is what He always desires.

In the prayer Jesus taught His disciples to pray, He began by teaching them to pray, *"Our Father in heaven, hallowed be Your name"* (Matt. 6:9). When we say the words, "hallowed be Your name," we are declaring that His nature, character, personality, and attributes are unlike any other earthly expression. In other words, nothing is better than our Father in Heaven.

I like to compare this to the difference between Spam and filet mignon. Our Father in Heaven is like a perfectly seasoned and cooked filet mignon. Even the best father on earth is like Spam in comparison. Some people love Spam, because it is all they have ever tasted. Some choose to eat Spam because they cannot afford filet mignon, and so have adjusted their taste accordingly. I have tasted both and have unequivocally concluded that filet mignon is "hallowed." It is set apart, consecrated, and holy. Nothing, especially Spam, can compare with filet mignon; it is on a whole different level.

So it is with the name of our Father. His nature, character, personality, and attributes are above anything of this world. So when we pray, "Our

Father in Heaven, hallowed be Your name," or when we pray for someone in the name of His Son, Jesus, we are praying that everything that expresses His name will be revealed, so that people see that He is incomparable. We are tapping into the attributes of the bearer of the name, obtaining His endorsement and power.

Endnote

1. *The New Testament Greek Lexicon*, Studylight.org, s.v. *ballo*, Strong's #906 (http://www.searchgodsword.org/lex/grk/view.cgi?number=906) and *diaballo*, Strong's #1225 (http://www.searchgodsword.org/lex/grk/view.cgi?number=1225).

Points to Ponder

1. Have you added "in the name of Jesus" as a tag line to your prayers of petition? Most Christians have. Now is the time to graduate to a new level of understanding about why you pray in the name of Jesus. Now you no longer need to invoke His name just to make sure your prayer is "correct."

....

....

....

2. What is the meaning of your personal name, if you know? Look it up again to make sure. How can your own personal name carry a blessing?

....

....

....

Meditation

The Name speaks for itself, and it is all-powerful:

*God also has highly exalted Him and given Him **the name which is above every name**, that at the name of Jesus every knee should bow, of those in heaven, and of those on earth, and of those under the earth, and that every tongue should confess that Jesus Christ is Lord, to the glory of God the Father* (Philippians 2:9-11).

*Therefore I also, after I heard of your faith in the Lord Jesus and your love for all the saints, do not cease to give thanks for you, making mention of you in my prayers: that the God of our Lord Jesus Christ, the Father of glory, may give to you the spirit of wisdom and revelation in the knowledge of Him, the eyes of your understanding being enlightened; that you may know what is the hope of His calling, what are the riches of the glory of His inheritance in the saints, and what is the exceeding greatness of His power toward us who believe, according to the working of His mighty power which He worked in Christ when He raised Him from the dead and seated Him at His right hand in the heavenly places, **far above all principality and power and might and dominion, and every name that is named**, not only in this age but also in that which is to come* (Ephesians 1:15-21).

In the name of Jesus, Amen.

Chapter 37

Bringing Signs and Wonders to the Streets
Bill Johnson

J ESUS' PRIMARY MISSION IS summed up in this one line: *"For this purpose the Son of God was manifested, that He might destroy the works of the devil"* (1 John 3:8). That was Jesus' assignment; it was the disciples' assignment, and it is your assignment as well. God's purpose in saving you was not simply to rescue you and keep you busy until He shipped you off to Heaven. His purpose was much bigger; He commissioned you to demonstrate the will of God, "on earth as it is in heaven," helping to transform this planet into a place that is radiant and saturated with His power and presence. This is the very backbone of the Great Commission, and it should define your life and mine.

In our school of ministry we train people in signs and wonders, and we are especially keen to learn how to operate in the supernatural outside the four walls of the church. We encourage our students by giving them specific assignments to invite God to work in public places.

One day after class a bunch of students from our Worship School went to visit a lady in the hospital. She had a brain tumor, was deaf in one ear, and was losing feeling on the right side of her body. She spoke with great difficulty, slurring her words, and she was in terrible pain. Instead of laying hands on her and praying, the students surrounded her in worship, singing songs, expressing their love to the Lord. Pretty soon the woman said, "My ears opened!" The deafness had left. They kept singing and she said, "My speech is clearer!" She started speaking clearly. Pretty soon she was moving her limbs around. She exclaimed, "All the pain is gone!" God overhauled her body when a worship service broke out around her.

When we do the will of God, we bring Kingdom reality crashing into the works of the devil. We initiate conflict between earthly reality and heavenly reality, becoming the bridge that asserts, through prayer and radical obedience, the rulership of God.

Not long ago, a woman with a broken arm came to our church with her wrist in such pain that we couldn't even touch her skin to pray for it. We held our hands away and prayed, and within moments God healed it completely. She had no pain and was twisting the wrist all around. The arm was totally different than it had been seconds earlier. Kingdom reality had overwhelmed one of the devil's works. That's the normal Christian life.

Besides feeding the poor weekly, we have an annual holiday feast, in which families from the church adopt a table in our gym and decorate it with Christmas decorations. The tables are set with their finest china, crystal, and silverware. Then we bus the needy to this event held in their honor. This past year we served prime rib. We started with 34 roasts to feed two seatings of about 500 people each. After serving 19 roasts in the first seating, we realized that the 15 we had left were not enough for the 200 workers plus the second group of 500. The decision was made not to feed the workers. But when they went back into the kitchen, there were 22 roasts. Seven more had mysteriously appeared. The workers were then fed, as was the second group of needy people. That should have exhausted our mysterious 22 roasts, but there were 12 more left after everyone had eaten! Multiplying bread is great, but I really like seeing prime rib multiply!

Aren't you tired of talking about a gospel of power, but never seeing it in action? Aren't you tired of trying to carry out the Great Commission without offering proof that the Kingdom works? Too many of us have been like a vacuum cleaner salesman who comes to the door and throws some dirt on the floor and says, "I represent the WhizBang vacuum cleaner company. My vacuum cleaner is so strong that you will have to remove pets and small children from the room. It sucks up everything in sight." But instead of demonstrating the vacuum cleaner, he simply hands you a brochure (tract), promises that the machine will work, and walks away. That's cheating people! Yet that's often how we preach the gospel. We tell people how great the product is, but seldom demonstrate or prove it. It's like saying, "Hi! My name is Bill Johnson. I represent the King and His Kingdom. He heals all your diseases, delivers you from all your torments, and gets rid of the messes in your life. I can't show you how, though. You'll just have to believe it. So long."

Don't you think we have improperly defined how the Kingdom of God operates, missing the bulk of what Jesus taught? Some people teach that the Kingdom of God is for some time in the distant future or past, not here and now. Some consign all the promises of God in the Bible to the millennium or to eternity because the accepted wisdom is that we're going to barely make Heaven. But Jesus taught and demonstrated that the Kingdom of God is a present-tense reality—it exists now in the invisible realm and is superior to everything in the visible realm. In the same way that Jesus is fully God and fully man, so the Kingdom is fully now and fully then. He spent His ministry showing us how to bring Kingdom power to bear on the works of the devil. *Our ministry should do the same.*

We can't be self-commissioned, relying on our ministry gifts to carry out the Great Commission. We can't afford to work apart from the supernatural intervention of Kingdom reality. Our assignment has never been what we can do for God, but what God can do through us. Normal Christianity is living the essence of the gospel, doing what Jesus did and destroying the works of the devil.

Points to Ponder

1. How are you bringing the reality of Heaven, not just the doctrine of Heaven, to your neighbors or coworkers? How are you ushering in Kingdom reality wherever you go? How "normal" is your Christian life?

....

....

....

2. Do you know someone who is accomplishing the mission of the Great Commission—with success? The way you would measure success would be to take a look at the signs of the Kingdom: *The kingdom of God is...righteousness and peace and joy in the Holy Spirit*" (Rom. 14:17). How have righteousness, peace, and joy followed the actions of this person? What can you learn from him or her?

....

....

....

Meditation

The only way to do Kingdom works consistently is to view reality from God's perspective. That is what the Bible means when it talks about renewing your mind. The battle is in your mind, which God has appointed as the gatekeeper of the supernatural reality that He wants you to express to the world around you.

An unrenewed mind is of little use to God. It is like a discordant key on a piano that you learn to skip over because it detracts from the music. If you are out of sync with the mind of Christ, you will seldom get used, because your thoughts will be in conflict with the thoughts of the Lord. Far better to be in conflict with the world around you because you bring the Kingdom in and it clashes with the kingdom of darkness.

Set aside your preconceived notions. Ask the Lord to renew your mind some more today.

Chapter 38

STRENGTH FROM COVENANT PEOPLE
BILL JOHNSON

OUR CLOSE FRIENDSHIPS, ESPECIALLY those with our spouses, are powerful, because they are built on covenant. Covenant establishes an agreement that allows the spiritual reality that governs your life to flow to the other person, and vice versa. This is why it is so vital to develop friendships with people whose lives consistently display the fruit of the Kingdom. When we steward covenant friendships with people of faith, we stay connected to a growing source of strength that often greatly determines our ability to persevere through difficult times.

I am blessed to have close friendships with people of genuine faith. Time and time again I have been uplifted and strengthened simply by being with them. Often I'm not even able to mention the difficult situation I am facing at the time, yet I leave encouraged. There are several reasons for this. First, our love and honor for one another creates an exchange of life whenever we interact. Because my friends are people of faith, they naturally exude hope, promise, and joy. It doesn't take long when I spend time with them for me to benefit from their infectious attitude and good spirit. But best of all, covenant friendships, when they are built on knowing each other after the Spirit, have the effect of calling us back to our true identity in Christ. They refresh our connection to our purpose and to who we are in Christ, and when our vision for those things is renewed, usually our strength is renewed, too. For this reason, I know that one of the best ways to strengthen myself when I'm tired or discouraged is to grab hold of a friend and to spend some time with that person.

On the other hand, I have found that when I am in an emotionally vulnerable condition, or even if I happen to be just physically tired, I must be careful to stay away from people who like to complain or be critical. I have always had strong personal boundaries in place for discerning and limiting my interactions with people who speak from a heart of negativity or unbelief. Normally I will feel free to minister to such people, but I do not give them access to my life. When I'm lacking strength, however, I will intentionally avoid them. That may not sound very compassionate, but I am the only one who is responsible for keeping my heart free from doubt and judgment, and I alone can recognize when I am vulnerable to the influence of people who agree with those spirits. Solomon warned against the powerful effect of people's personalities and values when he wrote, *"Make no friendship with an angry man, and with a furious man do not go, lest you learn his ways and set a snare for your soul"* (Prov. 22:24-25).

Truth be told, not all ungodly counsel comes from the ungodly. While many people may mean well, they lack the faith perspective that I strive for, and they tend to work harder to make me more like themselves than they do to actually try to help me become stronger in my trust in God. My job is to protect myself from such an influence, especially when I am vulnerable.

My heart is a garden. Some people are good at planting weeds in it, while others plant the Kingdom there. My job, and yours, is to know the difference.

The gospels specifically mention occasions in which Jesus took His disciples away from the crowds to rest and be together. The testimony of revival history teaches us that very few men and women of God really learn how and when to do this. In case after case, the same person who carried a marvelous anointing that brought salvation, healing, and deliverance to thousands of people lacked the wisdom to see that he or she would not be able to sustain that ministry if he didn't learn to get away from the crowds long enough to get physical rest and to cultivate life-giving relationships with family and friends who could reaffirm his or her focus on the Kingdom. As a result, many of these revivalists died young and many of their family members suffered physically and spiritually.

We cannot afford to miss the lesson these stories teach us. If we are going to become people with whom God can entrust greater measures of favor and anointing to fulfill our purpose as a royal priesthood, we have to recognize that we are going to attract needy people. People's needs can exert tremendous pressure on us, and that pressure will expose the parts of our hearts that care more about meeting the expectations of others than doing only what Jesus is doing. In His ministry, Jesus met the needs of many people, but He also walked past a lot of other needy people. He understood that as one man, the only way He could succeed at what He was doing was to keep Himself in a position where what moved Him to action was not merely human need, but the actual heart of His Father.

The strength of our intimacy with the Father, Son, and Holy Spirit, and in the close, covenant friendships in our lives is what will largely determine our ability to minister from a place of strong faith and joyful obedience to God rather than from a place of striving to please or help people.

The people who are most vulnerable to overextending themselves on behalf of ministry relationships are the people who struggle with intimacy—both with God and with others. Ministry can be great for making them feel connected and loved, but the truth is, without the accountability that comes only from covenant friendships, they're just being set up for burnout or compromise. This is why God will pull many ministers out of ministry for a time just so they can learn how to be friends with Him apart from working for Him.

All true fruitfulness flows from intimacy with God.

Points to Ponder

1. Do you have close friendships with strong believers, friendships that you could term "covenant" friendships? Write down a few of the qualities that make these relationships unique. Decide how to nurture such friendships and/or how to develop them in the first place.

....

....

....

2. Name some specific ways that you have been helped in your walk of faith by your godly friendships. Name some ways that you have been hindered in your walk of faith by relationships with unbelievers or weak believers who operate out of their carnal minds.

....

....

....

3. If you were to die today, who would come to your funeral? What would they say in a eulogy about your legacy?

....

....

....

Meditation

Most of the people of faith who can make a consistent positive contribution to your life in times of need are also people with a great sense of humor. If you are the kind of person who resists laughter in difficult times, you need friends like these. It takes faith to be joyful in the face of a trial, and spending time with people you can trust enough to relax around helps you to foster the atmosphere in which laughter comes easily and often.

Odd as it may seem, sometimes you do not need to withdraw into your prayer closet or go on a retreat—you just need to tell funny stories, share joyful experiences, and learn to laugh at yourself. Friends of faith who can administer the good medicine of laughter are often just what the doctor ordered.

Remember that next time you need a friend, or when it's your turn to be a strong support to a friend in need.

Chapter 39

First Love
Banning Liebscher

I COULDN'T BELIEVE WHAT I was hearing. Elena, one of our high school campus leaders, was sitting in my office updating me on the campus ministry we had just launched. Her job was to activate Christian students to pray on her campus, and she was to gather other Christian students on her campus, challenging them to pray for five of their unsaved friends. Our goal was to see every unsaved student on the campus prayed for by name every week. Elena had connected with a handful of other Christian students and started organizing weekly prayer times. But a few weeks later, her Christian friends approached her, saying that they were no longer interested in praying and they were not going to attend the weekly prayer meetings.

When she told me this, I was stunned. I thought it seemed so *unnatural* for Christian young people—or any Christians, for that matter—not to be passionate about the things of God. More specifically, it seemed abnormal for Christians not to be passionately in love with God and, in turn, enamored with the things of God. Shouldn't passionate love be the primary characteristic of us as believers?

Unfortunately, much of the Church has promoted the idea that the hallmark of the believer's life is his or her ability to observe certain spiritual disciplines—to go to church regularly, to read the Bible, and to avoid doing bad things. But Christianity was never meant to be a life of disciplines. It was always meant to be a life of passion.

The most natural thing in the Christian life is to be passionately in love with Jesus and for this blazing love to infuse all that we are and do. In fact, as human beings, we were created to live passionately and are drawn to those who live with fervor. I believe we are attracted to passion because there is something within us that knows we were meant to give our lives for something greater than ourselves. Passionate love is really the only force strong enough to drive us beyond convenience and into sacrifice. Discipline will never be enough. Now, I'm a firm believer in disciplines and encourage Christians to embrace them, but they can never be the propulsive stimulus in our lives.

My marriage with my wife is not a marriage of disciplines. Although it would be untrue to say that every day of marriage is bursting with passionate love, I am married to my wife because I am fervently in love with her, not because I have entered into a business contract with her. It is true that love is a choice, not just a feeling I have, but I don't wake up every day saying, "Today, I'm going to choose to love my wife." My passion for my wife fills my heart and motivates me as I walk out my promise to spend the rest of my life with her.

One of the primary keys for sustaining an increasing passion for God is found in the book of Revelation. The apostle John, while in exile on the Island of Patmos, was taken to Heaven and came face to face with Jesus. In this encounter, Jesus gave John certain messages to write to various churches. The message He delivered to the church in Ephesus was that He saw their good works, but that He had one thing against them: *"Nevertheless I have this against you, that you have left your first love. Remember therefore from where you have fallen; repent and do the first works"* (Rev. 2:4-5).

I grew up in the church and have heard many sermons about this passage of Scripture. The message always went something like this: "When you are first saved, you were naturally on fire for God and you lived a life full of passion. You loved to pray, read your Bible, invite people to church, and witness. But eventually, as your journey took you farther down the road of the Christian life, your fire and passion for God began to diminish." In conclusion, we were always encouraged to return to our "first love" by remembering how we used to live as new Christians and starting to live that way once again.

To our credit, we would try to do this, but since we were performing out of duty rather than true passion, our efforts rarely produced the sought-after results and the attempt was always short-lived.

Here is a radical thought: I am not so sure that this passage means we need to go back to how we first loved Jesus. In another passage, John writes, *"We love Him because He first loved us"* (1 John 4:19). So I don't believe Jesus was telling the Ephesians to return to how they first loved Him; instead I am convinced He was telling them to *return to the revelation that He first loved them.*

It is the revelation of His love for us that awakens our love for Him. When you encounter His all-consuming love for you, the natural response is to fall completely in love with Him. His love incites our love to the point that we don't have to strive or struggle to live a life of passion. It just comes naturally.

Jesus taught his disciples: *"As the Father loved Me, I also have loved you; abide in My love"* (John 16:9). What a staggering statement! Jesus loves us the same way God the Father loves Him. There is no greater love than that. He then called us to *abide* in that love. He didn't tell us to try to recreate the love we used to have when we first got saved and then abide in our love for Him. Rather He wants us to abide in *His love for us.*

Every day of our lives, we get the opportunity to abide in the most extreme, zealous, over-the-top, wild, mind-blowing love imaginable. When we learn to do that, our natural response will always be extravagant love for Him in return.

Points to Ponder

1. Did this chapter change your interpretation of Revelation 2:4-5? (*"... you have left your first love. Remember therefore from where you have fallen; repent and do the first works."*) Now, what is your next step?

....

....

....

2. When did you first fall in love with Jesus? Was it a revelation of His love for you that made it happen? Has your experience of His love faded? Whenever it has been renewed, what sparked the renewal?

....

....

....

3. How do the Christian disciplines fit in with a life of passionate love for Jesus?

....

....

....

Meditation

Abide.

Rest. Trust. Rely. Love. Dwell. Enjoy.

Abide. Be refreshed. Dial down. Relax. Breathe. Be free.

Encounter. Engage. Expand. Tune in. Grow. Abide.

Abide.

Chapter 40

WELCOMING HIS VISITATION
BILL JOHNSON

HISTORY IS FILLED WITH people who prayed for a visitation of God and missed it when it came. This happened even though some had a strong relationship with God. Many believers have a blindness that the world doesn't have. The world knows its needs. But once many Christians are born again, they stop recognizing their need. There is something about desperation for God that enables a person to recognize God's move.

"Therefore let him who thinks he stands take heed lest he fall" (1 Cor. 10:12). Matthew says the *"dull of heart"* can't see (see Matt. 13:15). A dull knife is one that has been used. The implication is that the dull of heart had a history in God, but did not keep current in what God was doing. We maintain our sharp edge as we recognize our need and passionately pursue Jesus.

"First love" is passionate by nature, and it dominates all other issues in one's life. The Spirit of Jesus told the church at Ephesus that He would remove their "lampstand" if they did not return to their first love (see Rev. 2:5). While theologians don't agree on what that lampstand is, one thing is for certain: lamps enable sight. Without their lamp, the church in Ephesus would lose their perceptive abilities. Blindness or dullness is not always the kind that leads to hell. It just doesn't lead us to the fullness of God's intention for us here on earth. No first-love passion, no lamp.

Throughout Church history, those who rejected a move of God were generally those who experienced the previous one. Many decided they had "arrived." They felt they had experienced *the* move of God.

But God is a God of new things. Hungering for Him requires us to embrace the change brought on by His new things. Passion for God keeps us fresh and equips us to recognize a visitation of God, even when others reject it.

Being in great need enables a person to detect when God is doing something new. That great need doesn't have to be drug addiction or prostitution. Every Christian is supposed to maintain a desperate heart for God. We *are* in great need! Jesus addressed this fact with his words: *"Blessed are the poor in spirit, for theirs is the kingdom of heaven"* (Matt. 5:3). To be anchored to the center of His work, we must remain poor in spirit and consumed with a first-love passion for Jesus.

When the Church begins to look for the return of the Lord instead of pursuing a greater breakthrough in the Great Commission, the blessed hope is turned into the blessed escape. To want Jesus to come back now is to sentence billions of people to hell forever. It's not that we shouldn't long for Heaven. Paul said that is a comfort for the Christian. But to seek for an immediate end of all things is to pronounce judgment on all of humanity outside of Christ. Even Paul didn't want to return to Corinth until their obedience was complete. Is Jesus, the One who paid for all sin, eager to return without that final great harvest? I think not.

I believe that the desire to go to Heaven now is actually the counterfeit of "seeking first the Kingdom." Many revivalists had such significant breakthroughs that they expected the Lord's return any day. As a result, they failed to equip the Church to do what they were gifted to do—and they touched multitudes instead of nations and generations. We must plan as though we have a lifetime to live, but work and pray as though we have very little time left.

Many church services are designed to be as inoffensive as possible, on the assumption that any use of the gifts of the Spirit will send people running, turning them off to the gospel. But they are already turned off. For the most part, expressive worship, ministry in spiritual gifts, and the like only turn off Christians who have had the unfortunate experience of being taught against them. And many of these same individuals warm up to such things when they face an impossible situation and need the help of someone experienced in the gospel of power.

The Church has an unhealthy addiction to perfection, the kind that makes no allowances for messes. This standard of perfection can only be met by restricting or rejecting the use of the gifts of the Spirit. The passage often cited is First Corinthians 14:40: *"Let all things be done decently and in order."* However, the "all things" phrase refers to the manifestations of the Holy Spirit. Therefore, you need to have some "all things" first before you have a right to impose order on them.

Keeping things tidy has become our great commission. The gifts of the Spirit interfere with the drive for order. But messes are necessary for increase. Proverbs 14:4 notes: *"Where no oxen are, the trough is clean; but much increase comes by the strength of an ox."*

How important is increase to God? Jesus once cursed a fig tree for not bearing fruit out of season! (See Mark 11:13-14.) A man in a parable was cast into outer darkness for burying his money and not obtaining an increase for his master (see Matt. 25:24-30). There is a big difference between orderly graveyards and messy nurseries.

We miss God when we live as though we have Him figured out. In fact, if we think we understand Him, we have probably conformed Him into our own image. To endeavor to know Him is to embark on an adventure in which questions *increase* rather than disappear. He's the One who always works beyond our capacity to imagine:

> *Now to Him who is able to do exceedingly abundantly above all that we ask or think, according to the power that works in us, to Him be glory in the church by Christ Jesus to all generations, forever and ever. Amen* (Ephesians 3:20-21).

Points to Ponder

1. What do you think of when you read the word *visitation*? Is the prospect of a personal visitation from Heaven welcome to you?

....

....

....

2. In the past, have you been a part of what could be called a true revival, a season of special visitation from God? How did this season end (if it has ended)? If it has ended, do you think you could revive the revival if you wanted to? Why or why not?

....

....

....

3. Reflect on the line, "No first-love passion, no lamp." How can you illustrate the truth of that statement from your own experience?

....

....

....

Meditation

Mary received a visitation from an angel. He brought her the most shocking announcement ever given to a person. She was to give birth to the Christ child.

Like Mary, people who experience spiritual encounters seldom have immediate understanding of what God is doing or why. Sometimes their closest friends want to put them away, declaring the move to be from the devil. Often they are viewed as part of a fringe element in the Body of Christ. Of course, stigma alone is no guarantee that what a person has experienced is a true move of God. But the embarrassing prospect of being numbered with heretics, or at least with the deceived, can be a deterrent to seeking a visitation from Heaven.

In your own pursuit of God, do not allow yourself to be distracted or deterred by such fears. Seek His face passionately. He will keep you secure:

Now to Him who is able to keep you from stumbling,
And to present you faultless
Before the presence of His glory with exceeding joy,
To God our Savior,
Who alone is wise,
Be glory and majesty,
Dominion and power,
Both now and forever.
Amen (Jude 24-25).

About the Authors

Bill and Beni Johnson are the senior pastors of Bethel Church in Redding, California. Together they serve a growing number of churches that have partnered for revival. Bill is a fifth-generation pastor with a rich heritage in the Holy Spirit. Beni oversees Bethel's intercessors and Prayer House, which makes supernatural connection with the Lord accessible to all. All three of their children and spouses are involved in full-time ministry. They have eight wonderful grandchildren.

Kris Vallotton is the author of four other books and an international conference speaker. He is the senior associate pastor at Bethel Church in Redding, California. He has been married to his beautiful wife Kathy for 32 years. They have four grown children and seven grandchildren.

Kevin Dedmon has a traveling ministry focused on equipping, empowering, and activating the Church for supernatural evangelism through signs and wonders, healing, and the prophetic. He earned a master's degree in church leadership from Vanguard University, and has been in full-time ministry for more than 25 years. He and his wife are part of Bethel Church staff in Redding, California.

Danny Silk serves as a senior management pastor at Bethel Church in Redding, California. He is a primary developer of the staff team and director of the church ministries, including the Transformation Center, city outreach, and Bethel's Healing Rooms. Danny and his wife, Sheri, are also the founders of Loving On Purpose, a ministry to families and communities around the world.

Banning Liebscher has been on staff at Bethel Church in Redding, California, for over 10 years. He and his wife Seajay are the directors of Jesus Culture, a ministry dedicated to mobilizing, equipping, activating, and sending a new breed of revivalist all over the world. These revivalists are encountering God, burning with passion for Jesus, being trained and equipped in the realm of the supernatural, and being sent into their city to minister in power. Prior to his current position, Banning was the youth pastor at Bethel Church and a lead overseer in the School of Supernatural Ministry.

Recommended Reading from Bethel

A Life of Miracles by Bill Johnson

Basic Training for the Prophetic Ministry by Kris Vallotton

Basic Training for the Supernatural Ways of Royalty by Kris Vallotton

Culture of Honor by Danny Silk

Developing a Supernatural Lifestyle by Kris Vallotton

Dreaming With God by Bill Johnson

Face to Face by Bill Johnson

Here Comes Heaven by Bill Johnson and Mike Seth

Jesus Culture by Banning Liebscher

Loving Our Kids on Purpose by Danny Silk

Purity—The New Moral Revolution by Kris Vallotton

Release the Power of Jesus by Bill Johnson

Secrets to Imitating God by Bill Johnson

Sexual Revolution by Kris Vallotton

Strengthen Yourself in the Lord by Bill Johnson

The Happy Intercessor by Beni Johnson

The Supernatural Power of a Transformed Mind by Bill Johnson

The Supernatural Ways of Royalty by Kris Vallotton and Bill Johnson

The Ultimate Treasure Hunt by Kevin Dedmon

Unlocking Heaven by Kevin Dedmon

When Heaven Invades Earth by Bill Johnson

Available From Destiny Image Publishers

IN THE RIGHT HANDS THIS BOOK WILL CHANGE LIVES!

Most of the people that need this message will not be looking for this book. To change their life you need to put a copy of this book in their hands.

> But others (seeds) fell into good ground, and brought forth fruit, some a hundred-fold, some sixty-fold, some thirty-fold (Matt. 13:3-8).

Our ministry is constantly seeking methods to find the good ground, the people that need this anointed message to change their life. Will you help us reach these people?

> Remember this—a farmer who plants only a few seeds will get a small crop. But the one who plants generously will get a generous crop. (2 Cor. 9:6)

EXTEND THIS MINISTRY BY SOWING
3-BOOKS, 5-BOOKS, 10-BOOKS, **OR MORE TODAY,**
AND BECOME A LIFE CHANGER!

Thank you,

Don Nori Sr., Publisher
Destiny Image
Since 1982